P9-DGV-218

P9-DGV-218

Reader's Digest

Popular Songs That Will Live Forever

Editor: William L. Simon
Music arranged and edited by Dan Fox
Editorial Associates: Mary Kelleher, Elizabeth Mead, Natalie Moreda
Art and Design: Karen Mastropietro
Editorial Contributors: Barrymore Laurence Scherer and Richard M. Sudhalter

THE READER'S DIGEST ASSOCIATION, INC.
Pleasantville, New York/Montreal

Copyright © 1982 The Reader's Digest Association, Inc.
Copyright © 1982 The Reader's Digest Association (Canada) Ltd.
Copyright © 1982 Reader's Digest Association Far East Ltd.
Philippine Copyright 1982 Reader's Digest Association Far East, Ltd.

All rights reserved, including public performance for profit.
Any copying of any portion of the contents of this book
without the consent of the publishers may be an infringement of copyright.

Library of Congress Catalog Card Number 81-84487
ISBN 0-89577-104-7

Printed in the United States of America

Index to Sections

Index to Songs

INTRODUCTION

Remember when your parlor piano had a bench stuffed to overflowing with music? When on a rainy afternoon or after Sunday dinner you could open the lid to discover treasures untold, stacked there waiting to be played? Stephen Foster, Irving Berlin, George M. Cohan. A volume of Debussy or Liszt. A copy of "They Can't Take That Away from Me," with Fred Astaire dancing across the cover. Collections of old campfire favorites bearing such titles as *Our Fondest Moments.*

The American piano bench is almost just a memory today, gone with the nickel candy bar, white buck shoes and sarsaparilla. It belongs to another way of life, now fading fast even from memory as the last generations that remember it begin, inevitably, to gray at the temples.

Part of the remembered joy of such days — and, in particular, part of the pleasure associated with the piano and all those riches cached in the piano bench — was the thrill of discovery. We weren't quite so blasé then; American life didn't yet know the numbing predictability of a TV situation comedy or an assembly-line hamburger. There were still surprises, and it was still possible to savor small satisfactions.

One of them, now sorely missed, is the image of the family grouped around the piano, laughing while playing and singing old favorites, sorting through the stacks of sheet music and songbooks, whooping in delight when a familiar tune or fondly remembered lullaby turned up.

Images fade with their realities. But the spirit of such times remains, lovingly preserved between the covers of books such as this one. The seventh of the Reader's Digest songbooks, *Popular Songs That Will Live Forever* brings together a wide assortment of treasured songs — show and movie songs; hits from the turn of the century to the present; international standards; devotional classics and gems from operettas; even favorites from the world of jazz — creating a present-day "piano bench" full of times, places and memories.

With this book you can conjure up the flash and blare of "Seventy-Six Trombones," remember the sly wit of the great Fats Waller in "Ain't Misbehavin'," feel the first stirrings of love in "It Might As Well Be Spring" and share its triumphant declaration in Billy Joel's "Just the Way You Are," celebrate with the energy and joy of "Ain't We Got Fun?" and "California, Here I Come."

For the first time in any songbook or folio, you can also enjoy the perennials "Shine On, Harvest Moon," "Take Me Out to the Ball Game," "My Melancholy Baby" and "Twelfth Street Rag."

All 94 songs have been given sparkling, colorful new settings by Dan Fox, whose skillful arrangements have graced all our other music books. There are no finger-busting virtuoso passages, no dissonant "way out" chords. Yet the music is not obviously simplified either. Dan has created arrangements with rich, bright harmonies and a sense of rhythmic motion. Above all, the melody is triumphant, inviting you to sing and play — and have the time of your life doing it.

And the fun isn't limited just to pianists. Guitarists can play the songs from the melody line (the stems of the notes are turned up unless the line stands alone) and from the chord symbols or diagrams printed just above the staves. (It's worth noting here that Dan Fox himself is an accomplished guitarist — meaning that his voicings for that instrument have been done with particular resourcefulness and care.) Organists, too, will find much to savor. Pedal bass lines are given in small notes, with the stems turned down, at the bottom of the lower, or bass, staff. (These notes apply only to pedal organs; they are not applicable to the piano or to small, simple chord organs.) For the sake of facility, the bass lines move comfortably stepwise and stay within an octave. Players of C-melody instruments such as the violin, recorder, oboe, accordion and harmonica can read the melody from the top line as is. Those inclined to jazz improvising can use the melody and chord symbols to launch them into orbit.

Those same chord symbols can be the guide to pianists who have studied the popular chord method; they can read the melody line and improvise their own left-hand accompaniments. And they can provide a part for bass players, both string and brass; just play the root note of each chord symbol, except where another note is indicated (for example "G/D bass"). Accordionists also can use the chord symbols for the buttons played with the left hand; they can play the treble portion of each arrangement as written.

Dan Fox's harmonizations reflect the taste and sensitivity of a seasoned professional musician. Players and listeners alike may be surprised to hear how fresh and contemporary many of the arrangements sound — even with occasional echoes of such piano greats as Erroll Garner, George Shearing and Fats Waller.

So gather your family and friends around the piano or organ, lift the lid of the bench — or in this case the cover of *Popular Songs That Will Live Forever* — and begin to play. It won't be long before the singing starts. The years and the cares will roll away as the eternal magic of beloved music takes over. The treasure of the American piano bench of yore, the joys it represents, are yours forever.

— THE EDITORS

3

Send In the Clowns

from "A Little Night Music"
Words and Music by Stephen Sondheim

Stephen Sondheim's 1973 musical A Little Night Music, *an adaptation of Ingmar Bergman's film* Smiles of a Summer Night, *deals with a subject more suited to operetta than to the Broadway stage. Yet Sondheim's score is far from the sugary world of Sigmund Romberg or Rudolf Friml, and one song is hauntingly beautiful. "Send In the Clowns," sung in the show by Glynis Johns, became an instant classic in the way that songs from musicals used to but seldom do anymore. It is treasured by many performers, including singers Judy Collins and Sarah Vaughan.*

Copyright © 1973 Rilting Music, Inc., and Revelation Music Publishing Corp. (ASCAP). All rights reserved.

Ain't Misbehavin'

from "Ain't Misbehavin'"
Words by Andy Razaf; Music by Thomas "Fats" Waller and Harry Brooks

Fats Waller is reputed to have dashed off "Ain't Misbehavin'" in 45 minutes. But, almost always broke, he sold it even faster. In one moment of desperation, he sold his rights to it, and to 18 other songs, for $500. Louis Armstrong introduced "Ain't Misbehavin'" in a 1929 Broadway revue, Hot Chocolates. It showed up again on Broadway in 1978 in Ain't Misbehavin', a show composed of music associated with pianist-composer Waller.

Copyright © 1929 Mills Music, Inc. Copyright renewed, assigned to Chappell & Co., Inc. (Intersong Music, publisher) and Mills Music, Inc. International Copyright secured. All rights reserved. Used by permission.

Try to Remember

from "The Fantasticks"

Words by Tom Jones; Music by Harvey Schmidt

What keeps one show running to delighted capacity audiences for more than two decades at the same Greenwich Village playhouse? Whatever it is, The Fantasticks has it. Its fairy-tale love story and memorable score, featuring "Soon It's Gonna Rain," "They Were You" and, perhaps best of all, "Try to Remember," have helped make the musical a legend in its own time. Although the show opened in 1960, it wasn't until 1965 that "Try to Remember" became popular via a best-selling recording by Ed Ames.

Copyright © 1960 Tom Jones and Harvey Schmidt. Chappell & Co., Inc., owner of publication and allied rights. International Copyright secured. All rights reserved. Used by permission.

If Ever I Would Leave You

from "Camelot"

Words by Alan Jay Lerner; Music by Frederick Loewe

Camelot *was Alan Jay Lerner and Frederick Loewe's 1960 musical retelling of the legendary King Arthur-Queen Guinevere-Sir Lancelot romantic triangle. In the original production, it was Julie Andrews who had to make the difficult decision in choosing between Richard Burton, as Arthur, and Robert Goulet, as Lancelot—though her final choice of Mr. Goulet seemed almost inevitable after he sang the ardent, poetic declaration, "If Ever I Would Leave You."*

Slowly and somewhat freely

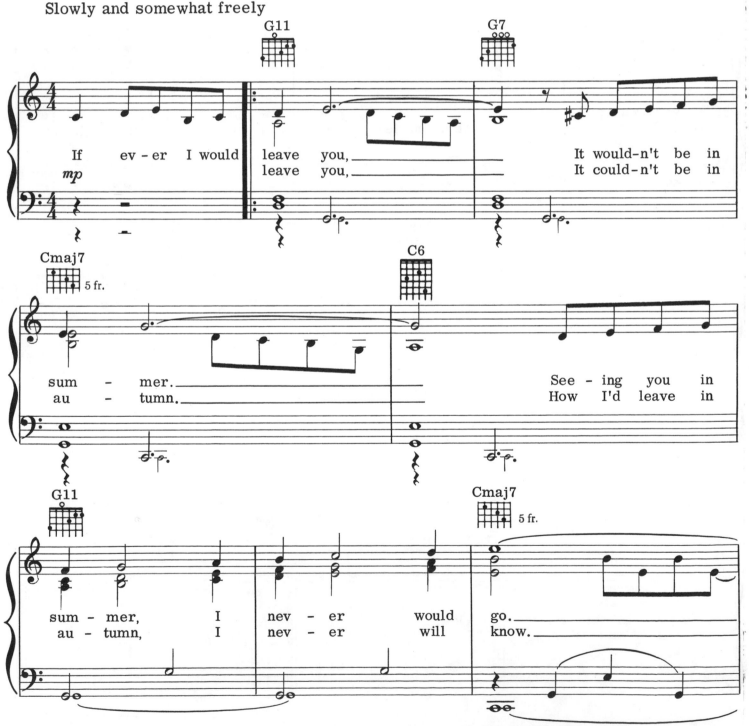

If ev - er I would leave you, _____ It would-n't be in
leave you, _____ It could-n't be in

sum - mer. _____ See - ing you in
au - tumn. _____ How I'd leave in

sum - mer, I nev - er would go. _____
au - tumn, I nev - er will know. _____

Copyright © 1960 Alan Jay Lerner and Frederick Loewe. Chappell & Co., Inc.,
owner of publication and allied rights throughout the world.
International Copyright secured. All rights reserved. Used by permission.

Your hair streaked with sun - light,____ Your lips red as
I've seen how you spar - kle____ When fall nips the

flame,____ Your face with a lus - ter____
air.____ I know you in au - tumn,____

1.
____ that puts gold to shame!____ But if I'd ev - er

2.
____ and I must be there. And could I
mf

Till There Was You

from "The Music Man"
Words and Music by Meredith Willson

Meredith Willson spent five years writing and rewriting The Music Man — 32 drafts no less — before he finally got his musical produced in 1957. For a while after the show opened, with Robert Preston in the title role and Barbara Cook as Marian Paroo, River City's librarian, "Till There Was You" was more or less overlooked in the furor over "Seventy-Six Trombones" (see page 18) and some of the other hits in Willson's score. In this tender song, the demure Marian tells how she failed to appreciate the beauty and enjoyment in everyday things before love for the strutting, baton-twirling Music Man opened her eyes.

bells on the hill, But I nev-er heard them ring-ing; No, I
birds in the sky, But I nev-er saw them wing-ing; No, I

nev-er heard them at all Till there was you.
nev-er saw them at all Till there was

There were

Copyright © 1950, 1957 Frank Music Corp. and Rinimer Corporation. Copyright © renewed 1979 Frank Music Corp. and Rinimer Corporation. International Copyright secured. All rights reserved.

Seventy-Six Trombones

from "The Music Man"
Words and Music
by Meredith Willson

Ever since Meredith Willson wrote this rousing march for The Music Man in 1957, school bands have been blaring it out at Saturday afternoon football games, circus clowns have been cavorting to its strains, and no parade is complete without at least one brass band strutting to its lively rhythm. "Seventy-Six Trombones," sung in both the stage and film versions by Robert Preston as the Music Man, "Professor" Harold Hill, isn't just a standard; it has become a tradition. What probably started it all: In the early 1920s, Willson had played in the band of March King John Philip Sousa. In addition to this classic, Willson's score for The Music Man contains "Goodnight My Someone," the barbershop standard "Lida Rose," "Trouble" and "Till There Was You" (see page 16).

Brisk march

Sev-en-ty-
six trom-bones led the big pa-rade,— With a hun-dred and ten cor-
six trom-bones led the big pa-rade,— When the or-der to march rang

nets close at hand.— They were fol-lowed by rows and rows of the
out loud and clear,— Start-ing off with a big bang-bong on a

Copyright © 1957 Frank Music Corp. and Rinimer Corporation.
International Copyright secured. All rights reserved.

finest vir-tu-o-sos, The cream of ev-'ry fa-mous band.____

Chi - nese gong, By a big bang - bong-er at the rear.____

____ Sev-en-ty-six trom - bones caught the morn-ing sun,____ With a hun-dred and

____ Sev-en-ty-six trom - bones hit the coun-ter-point,____ While a hun-dred and

ten cor - nets right be - hind.____ There were more than a

ten cor - nets played the air.____ Then I mod-est-ly

thou - sand reeds spring-ing up like weeds; There were

took my place as the one and on - ly bass, And I *(to Fine)*

say. There were fif- ty mount-ed can-non in the bat-ter-y,___

Thun-der-ing, thun-der-ing, loud- er than be- fore.

Clar- i- nets of ev - 'ry size and trum-pet-ers who'd im - pro-vise A

full oc - tave high- er than the score.

D.S. al Fine 𝄋

Sev- en- ty-

Bidin' My Time

from "Girl Crazy"
Words by Ira Gershwin; Music by George Gershwin

The Gershwins' 1930 musical Girl Crazy centered around the misadventures of a Park Avenue playboy out to make his way in Arizona. In keeping with the locale was the Western-style "Bidin' My Time," sung by a foursome who accompanied themselves on harmonica, Jew's harp, ocarina and tin flute. Girl Crazy gave a healthy boost to the careers of two young actresses: Ginger Rogers, who sang "Embraceable You" and "But Not for Me," and newcomer Ethel Merman, who stunned Broadway when she belted out "I Got Rhythm." Despite the musical's Western theme, the orchestra featured a roster of jazz greats who had not yet gotten started on their own, including Benny Goodman, Gene Krupa, Jimmy Dorsey, Glenn Miller, Jack Teagarden and Red Nichols.

Copyright © 1930 New World Music Corporation. Copyright renewed. All rights reserved

Oh Lady, Be Good

from "Lady Be Good"

Besides being the first successful collaboration by George and Ira Gershwin, Lady Be Good was the first Broadway hit to star the brilliant brother-sister team of Fred and Adele Astaire. In addition, the 1924 musical included "Fascinating Rhythm" and, of course, "Oh Lady, Be Good," which was sung in the show (to a chorus of flappers) as a gentle, graceful melody. Today, it is usually given a bright, up-tempo treatment, as in this arrangement.

Words by Ira Gershwin; Music by George Gershwin

Moderate swing

Oh, sweet and love - ly la - dy, be good!_____ Oh,
I am so awf' - ly mis - un - der - stood; So,

la - dy, be good_____ to me!
la - dy, be good_____ to

Copyright © 1924 New World Music Corporation. Copyright renewed. All rights reserve

ALMOST LIKE BEING IN LOVE

from "Brigadoon"
Words by Alan Jay Lerner; Music by Frederick Loewe

As a team, lyricist Alan Jay Lerner and composer Frederick Loewe scored their first commercial success in 1947 with Brigadoon, *preceding* Paint Your Wagon, My Fair Lady *and* Camelot. *This charming fantasy of a Scottish village that wakens out of the mists for one day every hundred years proved the pair to be worthy of Broadway and gave the world such lovely music as "The Heather on the Hill," "Come to Me, Bend to Me," "There But for You Go I" and the now-classic "Almost Like Being in Love." The last lyrical number is sung in the show by the American hero Tommy Albright, who falls in love with a lass from Brigadoon — and, in a happy ending, remains with his love in the sleeping village.*

Copyright © 1947, renewed 1975 Frederick Loewe and Alan Jay Lerner.
World rights assigned to and controlled by United Artists
Music Company, Inc. International Copyright secured. All rights reserved.

Some Enchanted Evening

from "South Pacific"

South Pacific, *Rodgers and Hammerstein's 1949 musical, was based on some of James Michener's* Tales of the South Pacific. *The show's unusual hero was a middle-aged French planter, Emile de Becque, played by 57-year-old Metropolitan Opera star Ezio Pinza. It was with "Some Enchanted Evening" that de Becque proclaimed his love-at-first-sight for U.S. Navy Ensign Nellie Forbush (Mary Martin). Nellie at first resisted de Becque's impassioned pleas, singing "I'm Gonna Wash That Man Right Outa My Hair," but it wasn't long before she was joyfully singing "I'm in Love with a Wonderful Guy."*

Words by Oscar Hammerstein II; Music by Richard Rodgers

Copyright © 1949 Richard Rodgers and Oscar Hammerstein II. Williamson Music, Inc., owner of publication and allied rights for the Western Hemisphere and Japan. International Copyright secured. All rights reserved. Used by permission.

TONIGHT

from "West Side Story"

Romeo and Juliet *in New York? Yes, when Leonard Bernstein, Stephen Sondheim and dramatist Arthur Laurents have anything to do with it — and so* West Side Story *was born in 1957. In the process, Shakespeare's Montagues and Capulets became feuding teen-age gangs, the Jets and the Sharks; the "star-crossed lovers," a New York boy named Tony and a Puerto Rican girl, Maria. And the balcony scene? It was played out — where else? — on a fire escape, with Tony and Maria singing ecstatically of "Tonight."*

Words by Stephen Sondheim; Music by Leonard Bernstein

Copyright © 1957 Leonard Bernstein and Stephen Sondheim. This arrangement
Copyright © 1982 Leonard Bernstein and Stephen Sondheim.

Tonight

Just One of Those Things

from "Jubilee"

Words and Music by Cole Porter

"Just One of Those Things" is anything but. It is one of those legendary songs written on the spur of the moment—written, in fact, overnight. When Cole Porter's musical Jubilee was being prepared for its Broadway opening in 1935, Moss Hart, who wrote the book for the show, suggested to Porter that a strong new song was needed for the second act. The composer agreed, and the next morning he appeared with a sheet of scribbled notes and sang for Hart the complete verse and chorus of "Just One of Those Things." There was one word, however, that gave Porter trouble. He spent days poring through thesauruses and dictionaries, but he could not find an adjective to go with "wings" until a friend suggested a word that had probably never appeared in a popular song: "gossamer."

Copyright © 1935 Warner Bros. Inc. Copyright renewed. All rights reserved.

PEOPLE WILL SAY WE'RE IN LOVE

from "Oklahoma!"
Words by Oscar Hammerstein II
Music by Richard Rodgers

Oklahoma! (1943) was the first collaboration of Rodgers and Hammerstein. And what a collaboration it proved to be! Besides the title song, "Oh, What a Beautiful Mornin'" and "The Surrey with the Fringe on Top," the new team produced "People Will Say We're in Love," in which the young lovers, Curly and Laurey, warn each other against any sign of affection lest people get the wrong — or right — idea.

With an easy lilt

Don't throw bou- quets at me; Don't please my folks too much; Don't laugh at my jokes too much; Peo- ple will say we're in love!

Don't praise my charm too much; Don't look so vain with me; Don't stand in the rain with me; Peo- ple will say we're in love!

Copyright © 1943 Williamson Music, Inc. Copyright renewed.
International Copyright secured. All rights reserved. Used by permission.

ALL-TIME HITS FROM FILMS

IT MIGHT AS WELL BE SPRING

from "State Fair"
Words by Oscar Hammerstein II
Music by Richard Rodgers

For the only film score that they wrote together—State Fair, in 1945—Rodgers and Hammerstein had to come up with a song for the heroine, Margy (Jeanne Crain), who is about to go to the fair but has the blues for no apparent reason. Lyricist Hammerstein decided that her problem was spring fever. His problem was that state fairs are held in the fall, not in the spring. His solution: a lyric in which Margy sings that, although it's autumn, her feelings tell her it might as well be spring. Set to music in less than an hour by Rodgers, "It Might As Well Be Spring" won the Oscar for Best Film Song of 1945.

Copyright © 1945 Williamson Music, Inc. Copyright renewed.
International Copyright secured. All rights reserved. Used by permission.

Some Day My Prince Will Come

from "Snow White and the Seven Dwarfs"
Words by Larry Morey; Music by Frank Churchill

Walt Disney broke new cinematic ground in 1937 with his first full-length cartoon feature, Snow White and the Seven Dwarfs. *The dubbed-in singing voice of the heroine belonged to Adriana Caselotti, who first sang the touchingly expectant "Some Day My Prince Will Come." Despite the fact that the song had been introduced in this fairy-tale atmosphere and was a waltz, it has become a standard among jazz musicians, including Dave Brubeck, Miles Davis and Bill Evans.*

Some day my prince will come; Some day I'll
Some day I'll find my love, Some one to

find my love, And how thrill-ing that mo-ment will be, _____ When the
call my own, And I'll know her the mo-ment we meet, _____ For my

Copyright © 1937 Bourne Co. Copyright renewed. This arrangement Copyright © 1982 Bourne Co.

Love Is Here to Stay

Words by Ira Gershwin
Music by George Gershwin

"Love Is Here to Stay" is the last song George Gershwin wrote. He was working on it for the score of the film The Goldwyn Follies when he died in 1937 at the age of 38. Vernon Duke, composer of "April in Paris," was asked to complete the melody, but all he had to work with was a 20-bar lead sheet that indicated only part of it. Fortunately, Duke was able to reconstruct the tune with the help of Oscar Levant, a close friend of Gershwin's, who remembered the harmonies of the song from hearing Gershwin play it at parties.

Copyright © 1938 Gershwin Publishing Corporation. Copyright renewed, assigned to Chappell & Co., Inc. International Copyright secured. All rights reserved. Used by permission.

Three Coins in the Fountain

from "Three Coins in the Fountain"

Words by Sammy Cahn; Music by Jule Styne

Three American women in Rome, three charming men, three love stories, three coins in the fountain—the Fountain of Trevi—to guarantee (legend has it) a return to the Eternal City. These were the elements of the 1954 film for which Sammy Cahn and Jule Styne wrote this Oscar-winning title theme. Sung on the sound track by Frank Sinatra, the song made the Trevi Fountain one of Rome's major tourist attractions.

Three coins in the foun - tain,
Three hearts in the foun - tain,

Each one seek-ing hap-pi-
Each heart long-ing for its

ness,
home;

Thrown by three hope-ful lov - ers,
There they lie in the foun-tain,

Which one will the foun-tain
Some-where in the heart of

1. bless?
2. Rome.

Which one will the foun-tain bless?

Copyright © 1954 Robbins Music Corporation.

48

49

TRUE LOVE

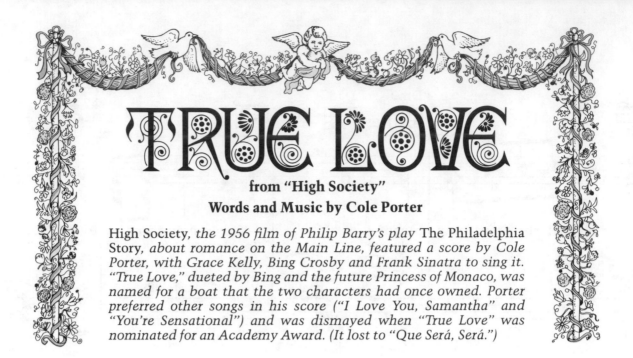

from "High Society"

Words and Music by Cole Porter

High Society, *the 1956 film of Philip Barry's play* The Philadelphia Story, *about romance on the Main Line, featured a score by Cole Porter, with Grace Kelly, Bing Crosby and Frank Sinatra to sing it. "True Love," dueted by Bing and the future Princess of Monaco, was named for a boat that the two characters had once owned. Porter preferred other songs in his score ("I Love You, Samantha" and "You're Sensational") and was dismayed when "True Love" was nominated for an Academy Award. (It lost to "Que Será, Será.")*

Moderate waltz

Copyright © 1955, 1956 Chappell & Co., Inc. International Copyright secured. All rights reserved. Used by permission.

WHAT ARE YOU DOING THE REST OF YOUR LIFE?

from "The Happy Ending"
Words by Marilyn and Alan Bergman
Music by Michel Legrand

Paris-born Michel Legrand and husband-and-wife lyricists Alan and Marilyn Bergman received their first Oscar in 1968 for "The Windmills of Your Mind," from The Thomas Crown Affair. *The following year the trio tried to repeat their success with "What Are You Doing the Rest of Your Life?," written for the ironically titled film* The Happy Ending. *(Ads for the film showed an anniversary cake dumped, untouched, into a liquor-bottle-filled garbage can.) Luck bypassed the trio in 1969, however: although "What Are You Doing" was nominated, the Oscar went to "Raindrops Keep Fallin' on My Head." But more gold statuettes were in order: to Legrand in 1971 for his score for* Summer of '42, *and to the Bergmans for "The Way We Were" in 1973.*

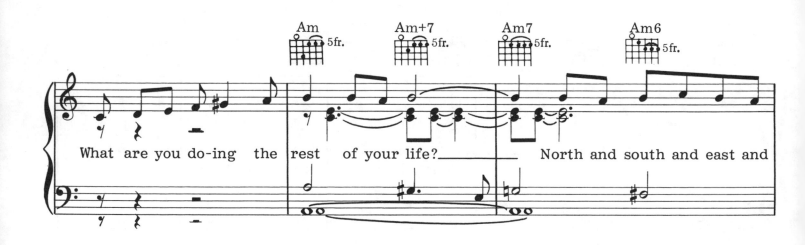

What are you do-ing the rest of your life?_____ North and south and east and

west of your life?_____ I have on-ly one re-quest of your life,_____

52

Copyright © 1969 United Artists Music Co., Inc.

from "Rosalie"
Words and Music by Cole Porter

"Rosalie," which Nelson Eddy introduced in the 1937 film of the same name, is proof positive that songwriters are not always the best judges of their own work. Cole Porter wrote six versions of it before producer Louis B. Mayer told him to forget he was writing for Eddy and to "go home and write a honky-tonk song." Although this final "Rosalie" became a big hit, Porter for years claimed that he disliked it and that the previous versions Mayer had thrown out were better.

Slowly, but not dragging

p getting louder   *little by little*   *slower*

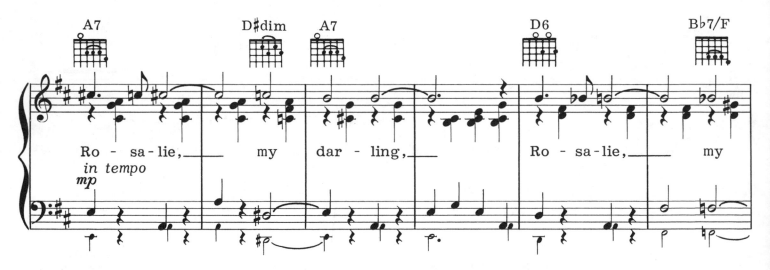

in tempo
mp

Ro - sa - lie,___ my dar - ling,___ Ro - sa - lie,___ my

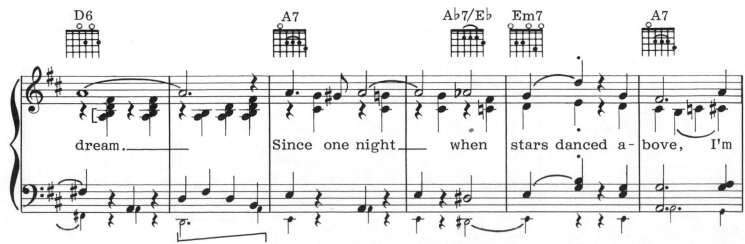

dream.___ Since one night___ when stars danced a - bove, I'm

Copyright © 1937 Chappell & Co., Inc. Copyright renewed. International Copyright secured. All rights reserved. Used by permission.

Lovely to Look At

from "Roberta"
Words by Dorothy Fields and Jimmy McHugh
Music by Jerome Kern

*The lovely Irene Dunne introduced "Lovely to Look At"
in the 1935 film version of Roberta, which also starred Fred
Astaire and Ginger Rogers. Jerome Kern, who had originally
written Roberta for Broadway with Otto Harbach, provided the
melody, and the talented and experienced songwriting team of
Dorothy Fields and Jimmy McHugh supplied the words. When Your
Hit Parade ("We don't pick 'em, we just play 'em . . . the top hits of the
week") was inaugurated on radio in April 1935, "Lovely to Look At" was
named the first No. 1 hit song in the nation. It was such a success that,
when a second version of Roberta was filmed in 1952, the producers
changed the title of the picture to . . . Lovely to Look At.*

Copyright © 1935 T. B. Harms Company. Copyright renewed. This arrangement Copyright
© 1982 T. B. Harms Company. International Copyright secured. All rights reserved. Used by permission.

Pick Yourself Up

from "Swing Time"
Words by Dorothy Fields
Music by Jerome Kern

Swing Time was one of the Fred Astaire-Ginger Rogers films that delighted moviegoers in the 1930s. Among the numbers in the film that the team danced and sang to was "Pick Yourself Up," in which Ginger struggled to teach Fred a simple step— if you can swallow that. Of course, with that pair, this sophisticated polka developed into a dazzling routine. Because of its clever key and rhythm changes, the song has become a favorite of jazz bands.

Moderately, with a lift

Noth-ing's im-pos-si-ble I have found, For when my chin is on the ground, I pick my-self up, dust my-self off, Start all o-ver a - gain.

Copyright © 1936 T. B. Harms Company. Copyright renewed. This arrangement Copyright © 1982 T. B. Harms Company. International Copyright secured. All rights reserved. Used by permission.

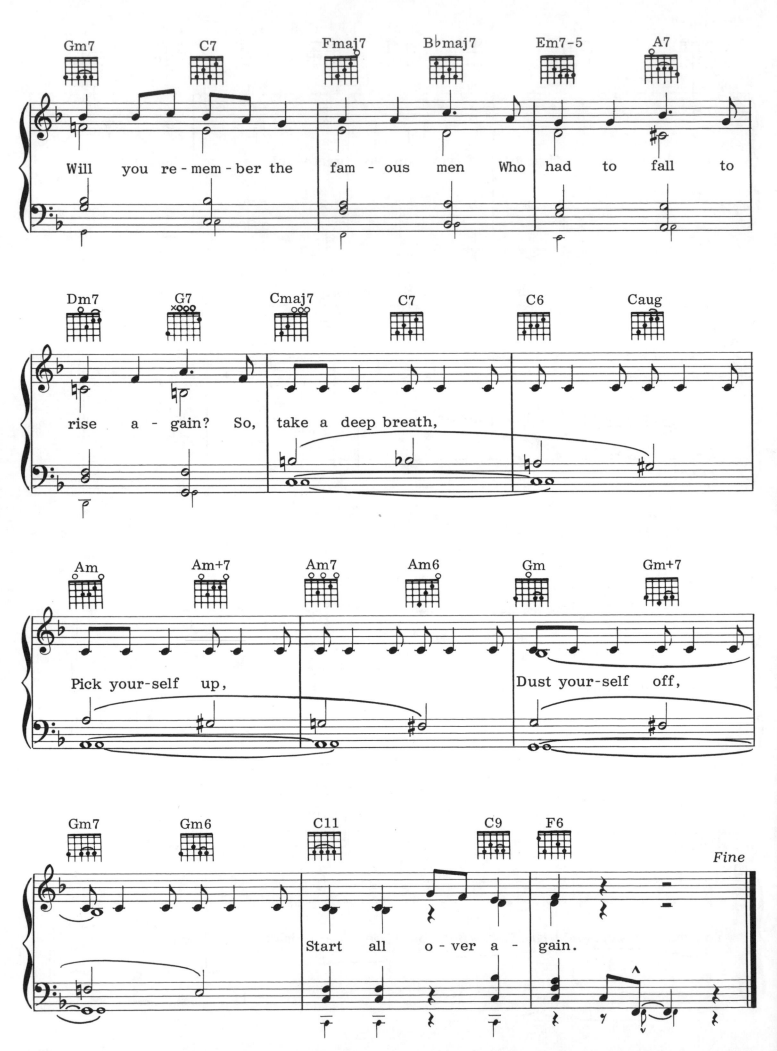

63

The Boy Next Door

from "Meet Me in St. Louis"
Words and Music by Hugh Martin and Ralph Blane

As one of the great movie musicals of the past, the 1944 film Meet Me in St. Louis lingers in the public's affections—not least for a score that produced several unforgettable songs, all closely associated with Judy Garland, who sang them in the movie. Among them are the title song (a tune revived from 1904), "The Trolley Song," "Have Yourself a Merry Little Christmas" and the wistful, reflective "The Boy Next Door." The last is a gentle little waltz, built around a series of unusual intervals; on paper, in fact, it might seem difficult to sing or play, let alone remember. Yet, like most enduring melodies, "The Boy Next Door" seems to sing itself, intervals and all.

Copyright © 1943, 1944 (renewed 1971, 1972) Leo Feist, Inc.

Theme from "A Summer Place"

Words by Mack Discant; Music by Max Steiner

The most remembered feature of the 1959 film A Summer Place, *which starred Richard Egan and Dorothy McGuire, is its "Theme" by Max Steiner, one of the giants of film composing (*Gone with the Wind, Now Voyager, *among others). Steiner's languorous theme for a languorous season provided a huge hit for orchestra leader Percy Faith in a recording that featured a piano. Later, in the '60s, two groups, the singing Lettermen and an instrumental quartet called The Ventures, also scored with the song. And every summer, somewhere, since it first appeared, the "Theme" seems to have a mini-revival.*

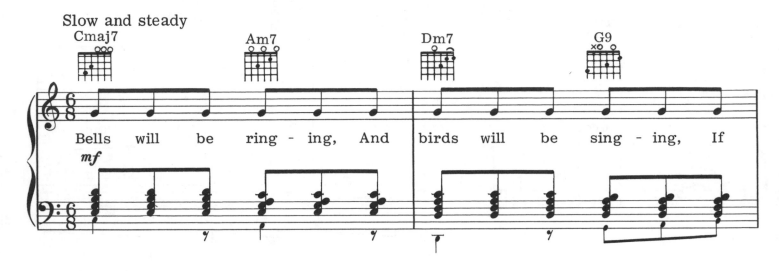

Bells will be ring - ing, And birds will be sing - ing, If

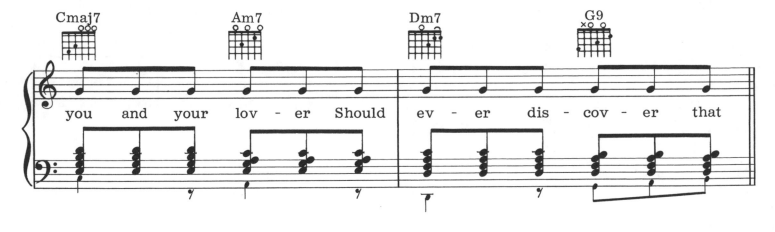

you and your lov - er Should ev - er dis - cov - er that

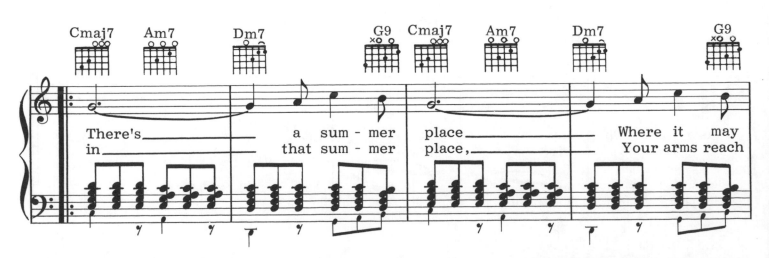

There's_____ a sum - mer place_____ Where it may
in_____ that sum - mer place,_____ Your arms reach

Copyright © 1959, 1960 Warner Bros. Inc. All rights reserved.

Theme from "A Summer Place"

SINGIN' IN THE RAIN

from "Singin' in the Rain"
Words by Arthur Freed; Music by Nacio Herb Brown

In 1952, Metro-Goldwyn-Mayer produced a film called Singin' in the Rain, *starring Gene Kelly, Donald O'Connor and Debbie Reynolds, with a score drawn almost entirely from earlier MGM musicals written by Arthur Freed and Nacio Herb Brown. Composer Brown had been a wealthy Hollywood real-estate investor before he turned to songwriting, while Freed eventually* progressed from songwriter to producer at MGM (he was *the producer of* Singin' in the Rain). *The two had written the title song, which provided a wonderful dance sequence for Gene Kelly, for* The Hollywood Revue of 1929, *a truly "all-star" show with, among others, Marion Davies, Norma Shearer, Joan Crawford, Jack Benny, Lionel Barrymore, Laurel and Hardy, and Buster Keaton.*

Copyright © 1929 (renewed 1957) Metro-Goldwyn-Mayer, Inc. All rights controlled and administered by Robbins Music Corporation.

HIT SONGS OF THE '50s, '60s AND '70s

Does the tale of an ex-convict riding a bus back to his home-town after three years in prison seem an improbable motif for a hit song? Well, just add the suspense of learning whether he'll find a yellow ribbon tied around the old oak tree—a sign that his love has waited for him—and you've got the best-selling record of 1973. (Tony Orlando and Dawn sold 5½ million copies alone!) Since then, over 400 recordings have been made of the song, which became the American theme of hope during the Iranian hostage crisis of 1979-81.

TIE A YELLOW RIBBON ROUND THE OLE OAK TREE

Words and Music by Irwin Levine and L. Russell Brown

Moderately, in 2 ($\half$ = 1 beat)

I'm com-in' home; I've done my time.
Bus driv-er, please,___ Look for me,

Now I've got to know What is and is-n't mine.
'Cause I could-n't bear To see what I___ might see.

If I'm

Copyright © 1972 Levine & Brown Music Inc. All rights reserved. Used by permission.

you re-ceived my let-ter, Tell-in' you I'd soon be free,
real-ly still in pris-on, And my love she holds the key, A

Then you'll know just what to do__ If you still want me,
sim-ple yel-low rib-bon's what__ I need to set me free. I

If you still want me.
wrote you and told her, please,

Chorus

Tie a yel-low rib-bon round the ole oak tree; It's been

IT'S ALL IN THE GAME

Words by Carl Sigman
Music by Charles Gates Dawes

When Tommy Edwards made "It's All in the Game" a hit in 1951, only the title and lyrics by Carl Sigman were new. The melody was written in 1912 by General Charles Gates Dawes, the future Vice-President under Calvin Coolidge. While commenting on the trials of love, the lyrics emphasize the power of true affection. Edwards revived the song in 1958, and other recordings were made by Cliff Richard in 1964 and Tennessee Ernie Ford in 1968. How's that for longevity!

Copyright © 1912, 1951 Warner Bros. Inc. Copyright renewed. All rights reserved.

Thornton Wilder's Pulitzer Prize-winning drama Our Town has become a basic fixture of classic American theater since its opening night in 1938, and once television arrived on the scene, it wasn't long before the play was broadcast. The 1955 TV production boasted musical numbers by Sammy Cahn and James Van Heusen, including the perky but sensible "Love and

Love and Marriage

Marriage." Introduced by Frank Sinatra, the song went straight to the heart of every viewer and later became the first popular song to win an Emmy Award. Its healthy, homespun sentiments also won it the religious Christopher Award. Play it and you'll understand why.

Words by Sammy Cahn
Music by James Van Heusen

Copyright © 1955 Maraville Music Corp., Los Angeles, California. International Copyright secured. All rights reserved.

Just the Way You Are

Words and Music by Billy Joel

The rise of Billy Joel from local Long Island entertainer to world celebrity has had a lot to do with his individual gift for writing memorable songs. In 1978 he wrote this graceful ballad as a birthday present for his wife, Elizabeth. Notable for its finely crafted melody, "Just the Way You Are" not only expresses tender love, but a hint of bitterness as well.

Copyright © 1977 Impulsive Music and April Music Inc. This arrangement Copyright © 1982 Impulsive Music and April Music Inc.
Administered by April Music Inc., New York, N.Y. International Copyright secured. All rights reserved. Used by permission.

Moments to Remember

Words by Al Stillman; Music by Robert Allen

A song can be nostalgic simply by association, such as a ballad that reminds you of your junior prom because it was a big hit that year. Other songs make a direct play for nostalgia—such as "Thanks for the Memory," "These Foolish Things (Remind Me of You)" or this great standard, "Moments to Remember." The song had plenty of competition back in 1955. Children's voices everywhere were piping "The Ballad of Davy Crockett," while adults marched along to Mitch Miller's rousing version of "The Yellow Rose of Texas." When the Canadian quartet known as The Four Lads recorded "Moments to Remember," however, the song skyrocketed up the charts, and the group had a million-seller on its hands. Not only was it one of the big hits of that year, but it later proved to be the song by which many of those growing up in the '50s now remember the decade.

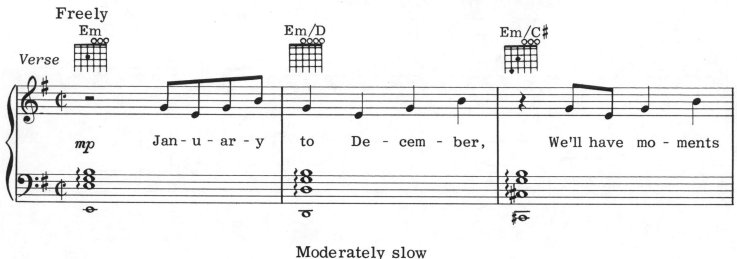

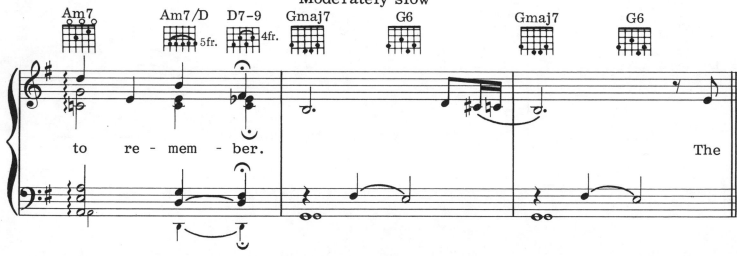

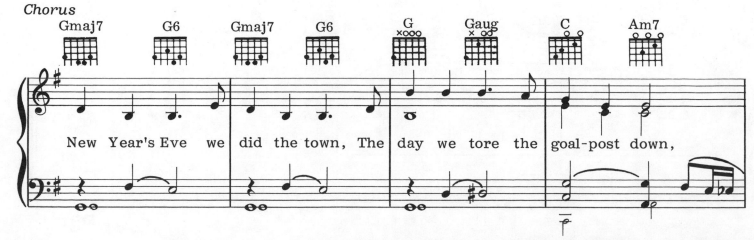

Copyright © 1955 Larry Spier, Inc., New York, N.Y. International Copyright secured. All rights reserved. Used by permission.

Moments to Remember

Spinning Wheel

Words and Music by David Clayton-Thomas

Although Canadian David Clayton-Thomas knew he had a hit song on his hands, the first company to record "Spinning Wheel" didn't think so. "It won't sell," they said, and refused to release the record in 1967. Eighteen months later, Clayton-Thomas's own rock group, Blood, Sweat and Tears, recorded virtually the same arrangement. Since then, the song that "won't sell" has sold more than 9 million recordings.

Moderately slow, with a beat

Copyright © 1968 Blackwood Music Inc. and Bay Music Ltd. All rights administered by Blackwood Music Inc. Used by permission.

Too Young

Words by Sylvia Dee; Music by Sid Lippman

No one ever seems to understand young folks, especially when it comes to affairs of the heart. "Too Young," introduced in 1951, said it all three decades ago and anticipated the current trend toward "instant adulthood." Johnny "The Creamer" Desmond, riding the crest of popularity he had gained as a crooner with Glenn Miller's Army Air Force Band during World War II, scored the song's first hit. But it was Nat King Cole's mellow voice that made it a big hit. Nat's record was his fourth million-seller in four years, following right on the tail of "Nature Boy," "Little Girl" and his terrific "Mona Lisa."

Copyright © 1951 Jefferson Music Co., Inc. Renewed 1979 Aria Music Co. All rights reserved.

"If" and the singer who eventually made it popular on this side of the Atlantic began their careers at the same time. The song was written in 1934 by three Englishmen. It became a hit in Britain that year but didn't catch on in this country where swing tunes, not dramatic ballads, were the rule. When *"If"* first appeared, 22-year-old Pierino Como had just made a difficult and fateful

decision. His barbershop in Canonsburg, Pennsylvania, was bringing in $125 a week, a lot of money in that Depression year. But Como was a singing barber, and he decided to take a chance and sing with a band for $28 a week. By 1950, when Pierino (now, of course, Perry) recorded *"If"* and made it a hit, that chancy decision had made him one of the most popular singers in the world.

Words by Robert Hargreaves and Stanley J. Damerell; Music by Tolchard Evans

Copyright © 1934 and 1950, renewed Cecil Lennox Ltd., London, England, for all countries of the world.
Assigned to Shapiro, Bernstein & Co., Inc., New York, N.Y.

HARBOR LIGHTS

Words and Music by Jimmy Kennedy and Hugh Williams

Jimmy Kennedy and Hugh Williams, the British songwriting team that brought us "Red Sails in the Sunset," created another American hit with their hauntingly lovely "Harbor Lights." First sung here by Rudy Vallee, it became one of the most popular tunes of 1937. In 1940 it received a new lease on life when it was used as theme music in the superb film version of Eugene O'Neill's play The Long Voyage Home. *Who can forget John Wayne, Thomas Mitchell, Barry Fitzgerald and Ian Hunter gazing shoreward as their ship glides out into a sea churning with enemy U-boats? Words were unnecessary. The yearning melody of "Harbor Lights" was sufficient to convey the hopes and fears, the loneliness and courage of the men as they faced unknown peril and tribulation.*

Copyright © 1937 Peter Maurice Music Co., Ltd. Copyright renewed. Chappell & Co., Inc., publisher and owner of publication and allied rights for the United States and Canada. International Copyright secured. All rights reserved. Used by permission.

Feelings

Words and Music by Morris Albert

Along with "Send In the Clowns," "Feelings," a remarkable one-shot hit by a Brazilian singer and songwriter with a very un-Brazilian name, Morris Albert, was one of the most pervasively requested songs of the 1970s. Albert once thought that he would like to become a caravia ("beach bum" in Portuguese). But when his own recording of "Feelings" became a No. 1 hit in 1975, first in Mexico and then around the world, he became an international singing star instead.

Slowly, but not draggy

p very smoothly

(no organ pedals except where indicated)

Feel-ings,___ noth-ing more than feel-ings,___
Tear-drops,___ roll-ing down on my face,___

Piano R.H. 8va higher than written; singers and other instruments as is.

Try-ing to for - get my feel-ings of

Copyright © 1974, 1975 Editora Augusta Ltda., Saõ Paulo, Brasil. All rights for U.S.A. and Canada assigned to Fermata International Melodies, Inc., Hollywood, California. This arrangement Copyright © 1982 Editora Augusta Ltda. International Copyright secured. All rights reserved. Used by permission.

*Chords to be played finger style.

NEVER MY LOVE

**Words and Music by
Don and Dick Addrisi**

The turning point in the musical careers of Don and Dick Addrisi, who wrote "Never My Love" for The Association, came when they were fired by a television company. They had been writing music for the TV producers' shows and also holding auditions for new talent. One unknown group, The Association, impressed them so much that the brothers put up $1200 of the producers' money to get instruments for the group. As a result, they were fired. Undaunted, they began writing songs, such as this one, that helped give The Association its start. Soon they began to write songs to give themselves a start as successful performers. The rest is show-business history.

You ask me if there'll come a time
You won-der if this heart of mine

When I grow tired of you,
Will lose its de-sire for you,

Nev-er my love,
Nev-er my love,

1.
Nev-er my love.

2.
Nev-er my love.

*Organ pedal doubles lowest note of piano left hand except where otherwise marked.

Copyright © 1967 Warner-Tamerlane Pub. Corp. All rights reserved. Used by permission of Edwin H. Morris (Canada) Ltd.

HIT SONGS FROM THE '20s

COQUETTE

Words by Gus Kahn
Music by Carmen Lombardo and John Green

When Guy Lombardo and his band first played Chicago in 1928, brother Carmen needed some lyrics for a tune that he had written with Johnny Green. He phoned Gus Kahn, who agreed to help. Unfortunately, instead of working, Kahn played golf every day, and poor Carmen, a non-golfer, had to tag along. Then one night, Kahn telephoned Carmen to say that he had just seen Helen Hayes in her New York hit Coquette and dictated some lyrics over the phone. The song was introduced by The Royal Canadians two nights later. It was a hit, but Carmen never learned to like golf.

Tell me why you keep fool - ing,
Break - ing hearts you are rul - ing,

lit - tle co - quette,_____ Mak - ing
lit - tle co - quette,_____ True hearts

Copyright © 1928 (renewed 1956) Leo Feist, Inc.

Charmaine

Words and Music by
Erno Rapée and Lew Pollack

A sweet-scented breath of loveliness from the 1920s, "Charmaine" was written by Erno Rapée and Lew Pollack for the classic silent film **What Price Glory,** *starring Victor McLaglen, Edmund Lowe and the beautiful Dolores Del Rio. Theater pit orchestras, mighty Wurlitzers and countless honky-tonk pianos played it wherever the film was shown, while contented audiences hummed and whistled it into tremendous popularity. Later, during World War II, Harry James and his orchestra played it in the movie* **Two Girls and a Sailor,** *and in 1951 it rose to even greater heights via Mantovani's best-selling recording.*

Moderately slow

p delicately

*No organ pedal till ***

(Female) I
(Male) I

R.H.

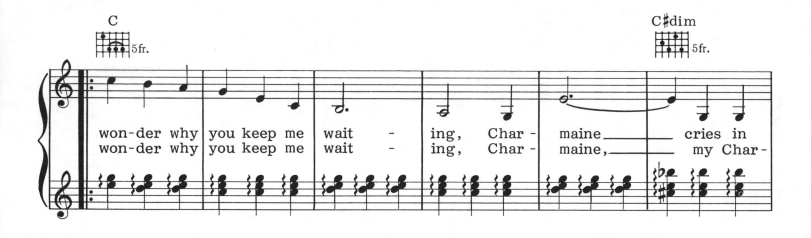

won-der why | you keep me | wait - | ing, Char- | maine_____ | cries in
won-der why | you keep me | wait - | ing, Char- | maine,_____ | my Char-

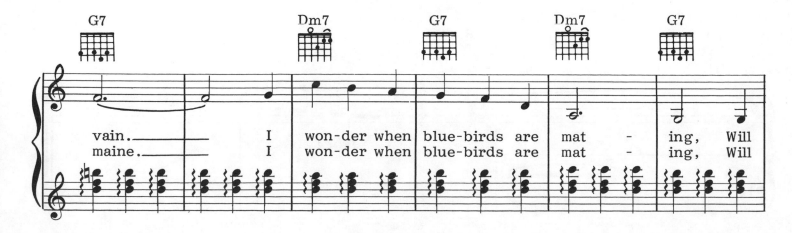

vain._____ | I | won-der when | blue-birds are | mat - | ing, Will
maine._____ | I | won-der when | blue-birds are | mat - | ing, Will

Copyright © 1926 (renewed 1954) Miller Music Corporation.

California, Here I Come

Words and Music by Al Jolson, Buddy DeSylva and Joseph Meyer

*When Al Jolson played in a Broadway show, he usually ended up
changing it entirely. This happened with Bombo in 1921, for which
Sigmund Romberg wrote 13 songs. Out they went, one by one,
as Jolson interpolated new ones: "Toot, Toot Tootsie! (Goo'bye)," "April
Showers" and "California, Here I Come." Although Romberg may not
have been too happy with the arrangement, Jolson's fans certainly were.*

Cal - i - for - nia, here I come, Right back

where I start-ed from, Where bow-ers of flow-ers

Bloom in the sun; Each morn-ing at dawn-ing,

Copyright © 1924 Warner Bros. Inc. Copyright renewed. All rights reserved.

BABY FACE

Words and Music by Benny Davis and Harry Akst

Harry Akst and Benny Davis collaborated on both the words and music of this 1926 Eddie Cantor hit. Akst toured in vaudeville with Nora Bayes, worked for Irving Berlin as a song demonstrator in the 1920s, and during World War II served as Al Jolson's pianist in the Pacific. Davis toured the vaudeville circuit as accompanist for Blossom Seeley. His other big songs include "Margie," "I'm Nobody's Baby" and that great favorite "Goodbye Broadway, Hello France." In a new disco version, "Baby Face" became a hit again in 1977.

110

Copyright © 1926 Warner Bros. Inc. Copyright renewed. All rights reserved.

Cecilia

Words by Herman Ruby; Music by Dave Dreyer

Dave Dreyer is responsible for several of America's most popular melodies, including "There's a Rainbow 'Round My Shoulder," "Back in Your Own Backyard" and "Me and My Shadow." "Cecilia" dates from Dreyer's days as staff pianist with the Irving Berlin Music Company. He had brought the song to Berlin, who liked it but felt it needed "an angle." All at once, Berlin thought of musically drawing out the second syllable of the name to make it "Ce-ceeel-ia." It was a stroke of genius, and it made Dreyer's song immortal.

Copyright © 1925 ABC Music Corporation. Copyright renewed. This arrangement Copyright © 1982 Bourne Co.

TOGETHER

Words and Music by Buddy DeSylva, Lew Brown and Ray Henderson

The collaboration of Buddy DeSylva, Lew Brown and Ray Henderson lasted only from 1925 through 1930, but those five years bore some extraordinary fruit: six Broadway shows, songs for five Hollywood pictures and nearly two dozen hit songs. Talk about togetherness! Moreover, each man was a hit songwriter on his own.

Their lovely waltz "Together," a 1928 success, was featured in the 1944 war film Since You Went Away. *(Remember Claudette Colbert and Joseph Cotten and cantankerous Monty Woolley up in the attic?) Its nostalgic quality of a peaceful yesterday gained it renewed popularity in a war-torn world.*

Copyright © 1927, 1928 DeSylva, Brown & Henderson, Inc. Copyright renewed, assigned to Chappell & Co., Inc.
International Copyright secured. All rights reserved. Used by permission.

Among My Souvenirs

Words by Edgar Leslie
Music by Horatio Nicholls

Sentimental songs that recalled the heart-on-the-sleeve ballads of the 1890s were extremely popular during the 1920s. This one—sentimental but not maudlin—was a 1927 collaboration by Englishman Horatio Nicholls and American Edgar Leslie, and enjoyed great success on both sides of the Atlantic. Years later, it was sung by Hoagy Carmichael in the 1946 Academy Award-winning film The Best Years of Our Lives, *and in 1959 a best-selling recording by Connie Francis made it a hit all over again. A good song certainly has staying power, doesn't it!*

Slowly and somewhat freely throughout

There's noth-ing left for me ____ Of days that used to be; ____ I live in mem-o-ry A-mong my sou-ve-nirs. ____ Some let-ters tied with blue, ____ A pho-to-graph or two, ____ I see a rose from you A-mong my sou-ve-

Copyright © 1927 Lawrence Wright Music Co., Ltd. Copyright renewed. Chappell & Co., Inc., publisher for the United States, Canada and South America. International Copyright secured. All rights reserved. Used by permission.

Ain't We Got Fun?

Words by Gus Kahn and Raymond B. Egan
Music by Richard A. Whiting

This tuneful song in praise of the joys of poverty has been a perennial favorite since it was written in 1921 by the team of Gus Kahn, Richard Whiting and Raymond Egan. Introduced during the heyday of vaudeville—when $10 was considered a good week's pay and the bill collector was a familiar if not quite beloved figure in the neighborhood—"Ain't We Got Fun?" was featured by such top-flight acts as Van and Schenck, who are also remembered for making a hit of "I Wonder What's Become of Sally" and many other numbers. Gordon MacRae revived the song in the 1953 film By the Light of the Silvery Moon.

Ev - 'ry morn-ing, ev - 'ry eve-ning, Ain't we got fun?

Not much mon - ey, oh, but hon - ey, Ain't we got fun?

The rent's un - paid, dear; We have-n't a bus.

Copyright © 1921 Warner Bros. Inc. Copyright renewed. All rights reserved.

Down by the O-HI-O

Words and Music by Abe Olman and Jack Yellen

During the 1920s, Tin Pan Alley songwriters, who rarely traveled more than two blocks from Times Square, revealed a surprising fondness for rural America. Two who did were Jack Yellen and Abe Olman, who wrote this paean to the Ohio River (Olman was born in Cincinnati, a city on its banks). Olman is known for "Oh Johnny Oh" and "Down Among the Sheltering Palms," while Yellen turned out "Ain't She Sweet" and "Happy Days Are Here Again," among others.

Copyright © 1920, renewed 1948 Forster Music Publishing Corp., Chicago, Illinois. Assigned to Cromwell Music Inc. 1979 and Jack Yellen Music 1979 in the U.S.A. International Copyright secured. All rights reserved. Used by permission.

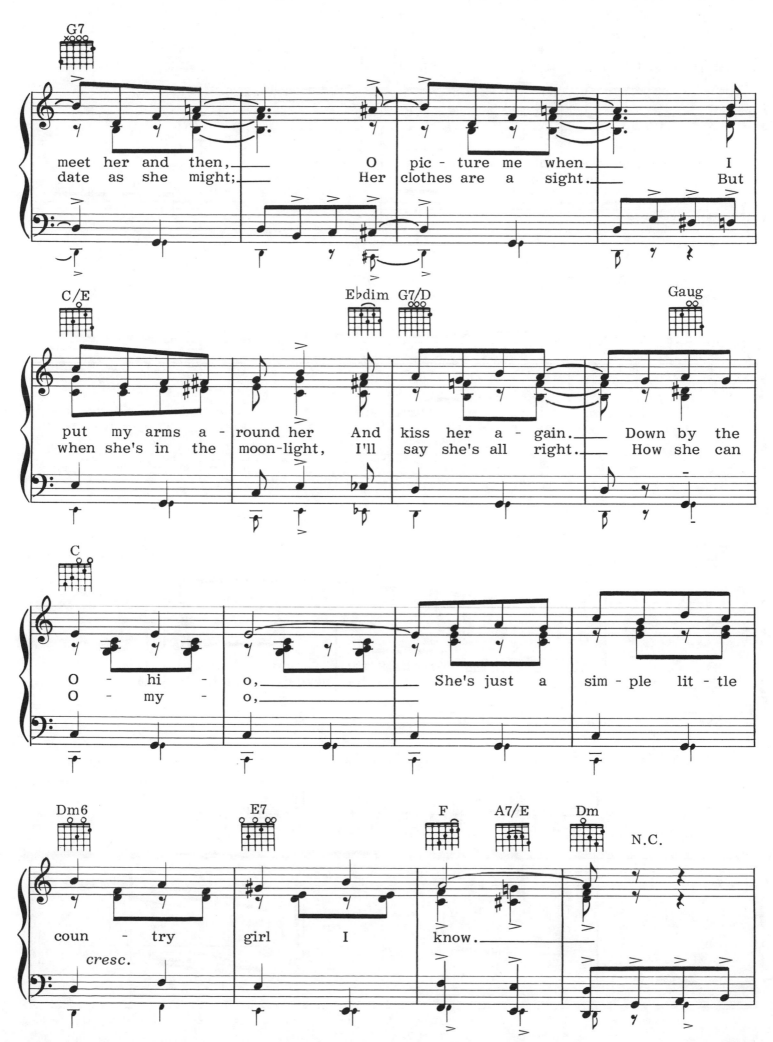

Down by the O-HI-O

THE VERY THOUGHT OF YOU

Words and Music by Ray Noble

Many Americans remember Ray Noble as the slow-witted Englishman he played for years on the Edgar Bergen-Charlie McCarthy radio show. Behind this façade lay a highly creative musician who led an English band in the early 1930s. When he came over here in 1934, Glenn Miller assembled an all-star band for him at the Rainbow Room in New York City and also arranged much of its repertoire. This song was the band's theme. Among Noble's other hits are "Cherokee" and the Rudy Vallée charmer "Goodnight Sweetheart."

Copyright © 1934 Campbell-Connelly & Co., Ltd. Copyright renewed. All rights for the United States and Canada controlled by Warner Bros. Inc. All rights reserved.

The Very Thought of You

DON'T BLAME ME

Words by Dorothy Fields; Music by Jimmy McHugh

For a song that has become one of the all-time popular favorites, "Don't Blame Me" got off to an unusually furtive start. It had been introduced by Jeannette Loff in the short-lived 1932 Chicago revue Clowns in Clover. The next year, the song was used as a promotional number for the film Dinner at Eight, although it was not heard on screen. For some reason it couldn't seem to find a niche of its own. Then Bing Crosby got hold of "Don't Blame Me" and rescued it from its relative obscurity. Since then, it has survived and has been sung and played year after year after year.

Slowly and somewhat freely

Copyright © 1932 (renewed 1960) Robbins Music Corporation.

ALL OF ME

**Words and Music by
Seymour Simons
and Gerald Marks**

For Seymour Simons, "All of Me" was just one of many song hits that he wrote while leading his own orchestra in Detroit in the early '30s. But for Gerald Marks, his collaborator, it was the start of a songwriting career that was to earn him citations from all over the U.S.A. Belle Baker introduced the song on radio in 1931, and it was featured the next year in the Joan Bennett film Careless Lady. In 1952, Frank Sinatra made it a hit again in the film Meet Danny Wilson. For a while, jazzmen tended to swing the tune and up the tempo, but in 1980, Willie Nelson revived the original ballad approach.

Copyright © 1931 Bourne Co. Copyright renewed. This arrangement Copyright © 1982 Bourne Co.

COCKTAILS FOR TWO

Words and Music by Arthur Johnston and Sam Coslow

Like the socialite character played by Margaret Dumont in many Marx Brothers pictures, the sophistication to which this song seems to aspire is always being deflated. "Cocktails for Two" was written for a 1934 film, Murder at the Vanities, that dealt with a fictitious backstage murder at Earl Carroll's Vanities—an annual Broadway revue in the '30s. Unfortunately, the backdrop for the number was so heavily laden with art deco chrome and glass that it distracted from the intimate charm of the gentle tune. Then the song re-emerged a decade later, manhandled by the incorrigible Spike Jones and His City Slickers, in an ear-splitting arrangement that featured gunshots, hiccups, gulps and shattering glasses. Now, however, in the peace and privacy of your own home, you can dim the lights, pour a couple of cocktails and perform the song in the seductive manner it has deserved all along.

In some se - clud - ed ren - dez- vous_____
rette_____

That o - ver - looks the av - e - nue,_____
To some ex - qui - site chan - son- nette,_____

Copyright © 1934, renewed 1961 Famous Music Corporation. This arrangement Copyright © 1982 by Famous Music Corporation.

With some-one shar-ing a de-light-ful chat Of this and that And
Two hands are sure to sly-ly meet be-neath A ser-vi-ette And With

cock-tails for two.

As we en-joy a cig-a-

cock-tails for two.

My head may go reel - ing,

But my heart will be o-

be - di-ent,

With in-tox-i-cat-ing kiss-es

For the

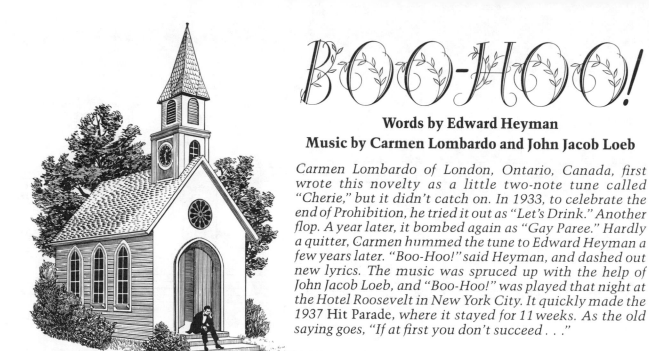

BOO-HOO!

Words by Edward Heyman
Music by Carmen Lombardo and John Jacob Loeb

Carmen Lombardo of London, Ontario, Canada, first wrote this novelty as a little two-note tune called "Cherie," but it didn't catch on. In 1933, to celebrate the end of Prohibition, he tried it out as "Let's Drink." Another flop. A year later, it bombed again as "Gay Paree." Hardly a quitter, Carmen hummed the tune to Edward Heyman a few years later. "Boo-Hoo!" said Heyman, and dashed out new lyrics. The music was spruced up with the help of John Jacob Loeb, and "Boo-Hoo!" was played that night at the Hotel Roosevelt in New York City. It quickly made the 1937 Hit Parade, where it stayed for 11 weeks. As the old saying goes, "If at first you don't succeed . . ."

Copyright © 1936 Shapiro, Bernstein & Co. Inc., renewed 1964 Ahlert-Burke Corp. for U.S.A. only.

hoo, _____

That's why I'm

cry - ing for you. _____

Some - day you'll feel like I do, and

you'll Be boo - hoo - hoo - in' too.

When I Grow Too Old to Dream

Words by Oscar Hammerstein II; Music by Sigmund Romberg

*The success of this tender waltz — first sung by that idol
of the silents Ramon Novarro in the 1935 film
The Night Is Young — came as a surprise to its lyricist
Oscar Hammerstein II. He felt that the opening lines —
"When I grow too old to dream, I'll have you to remember" —
didn't quite make sense, but he loved them; they felt
right. But what did they mean? Nevertheless, it
soon became apparent that the public had accepted the words
in the special sense that when a person grows too
old to dream of a future love, he can still recall a love of the
past. This had been Hammerstein's subconscious meaning all along.*

Slowly and simply

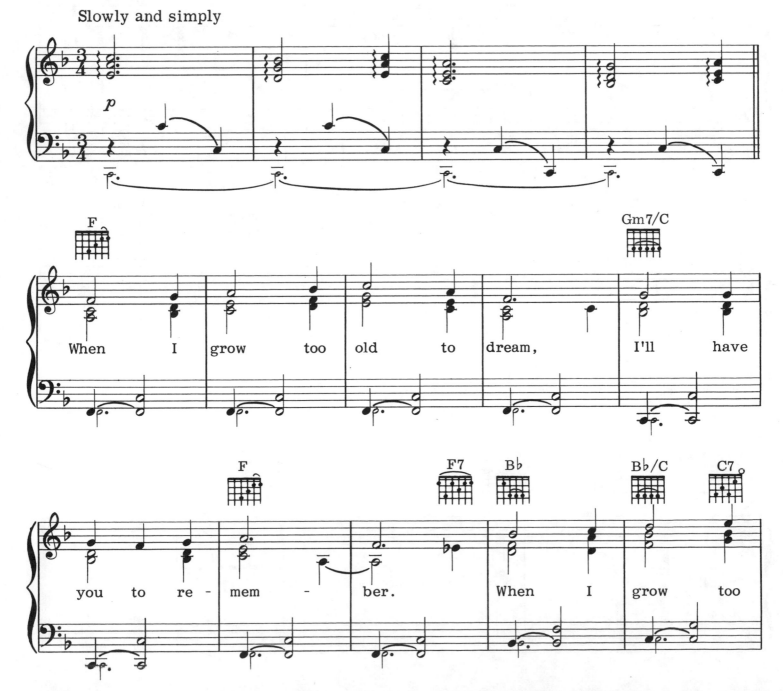

When I grow too old to dream, I'll have
you to re-mem-ber. When I grow too

Copyright © 1934, 1935 (renewed 1962, 1963) Metro-Goldwyn-Mayer, Inc. Rights throughout the world controlled by Robbins Music Corporation.

ISLE OF CAPRI

Words by Jimmy Kennedy; Music by Will Grosz

Romantic and nostalgic, with an amusing twist at the end, "Isle of Capri" is a product of the famed British songwriting team of Will Grosz and Jimmy Kennedy. Guy Lombardo and His Royal Canadians introduced the ballad in the U.S.A. in 1934, and Xavier Cugat and his orchestra popularized it further through their nightclub appearances and recordings. But it was the raucous swing version by Wingy Manone in 1935 that brought the song its greatest fame and gave the one-armed trumpeter his first hit recording.

Copyright © 1934, renewed and assigned to T. B. Harms Company and Anne Rachel Music Corp. This arrangement Copyright © 1982 T. B. Harms Company. International Copyright secured. All rights reserved. Used by permission.

STARS FELL ON ALABAMA

Words by Mitchell Parish; Music by Frank Perkins

Alabama, often referred to by its nickname, The Heart of Dixie, has inspired dozens of well-known melodies, one of which made a deep impression on the world of popular music in 1934. Without a doubt the most famous of Frank Perkins' compositions, "Stars Fell on Alabama" came out at the same time as Carl Carmer's popular novel of the same title, although there was no connection between the two works. Mitchell Parish, lyricist for a long list of songwriting greats, wrote the words.

140

Copyright © 1934 Mills Music, Inc. Copyright renewed. All rights reserved. Used with permission.

*Keyboard players let go of melody note to play final four chords.

LET'S FALL IN LOVE

Words by Ted Koehler
Music by Harold Arlen

This is a song that helped to change the direction of Harold Arlen's career as a composer. By the early '30s, Arlen was enjoying success writing songs for the revues at New York's Cotton Club — songs that had a tough, brassy quality suitable for nightclub presentation, such as "I've Got the World on a String" and "Between the Devil and the Deep Blue Sea." Following the success of their great hit "Stormy Weather" in 1933, Arlen and his lyricist Ted Koehler were summoned by

Columbia Pictures to write songs for the film Let's Fall in Love. En route to Hollywood aboard The Chief, they found themselves alone in the observation car. Soon a dining-car waiter passed through, striking the dinner chimes. Anxious to begin writing, Arlen prevailed upon the man to lend him the chimes, on which he quickly improvised a few notes of the film's title song. Within a few minutes, he and Koehler were hard at work with pencil, paper and chimes. By the time they arrived in Hollywood, "Let's Fall in Love" was completed. Written on those dinner chimes, the song kept the collaborators in cakes and ale for some time, and for the next 15 years, Arlen was primarily a film composer who turned out such hits as "Over the Rainbow," "Blues in the Night" and "That Old Black Magic."

142

Copyright © 1933 Bourne Co. Copyright renewed. This arrangement Copyright © 1982 Bourne Co.

TO EACH HIS OWN

Words and Music by Jay Livingston and Ray Evans

While Olivia de Havilland and John Lund were in the throes of filming To Each His Own—one of the four-handkerchief dramas of 1946—Ray Evans and Jay Livingston were writing a title song for the picture. Though it was never used in the film, "To Each His Own" said something special to battle-weary GIs returning from overseas. Its honest sentiment offered a welcome bit of musical philosophy for countless homecomings. Eddy Howard, the crooner whose band was a big favorite at Chicago's Aragon Ballroom, recorded the song, and it became one of his greatest hits. The Ink Spots also made a best-selling record of it. Livingston and Evans later scored with such follow-ups as "Buttons and Bows," "Silver Bells" and "Mona Lisa."

Slow and steady

Copyright © 1946, renewed 1973 Paramount Music Corporation. This arrangement Copyright © 1982 Paramount Music Corporation.

To Each His Own

It's Been a Long, Long Time

By 1945, people were beginning to see the light at the end of the dark tunnel of World War II. Popular songs, which had been promising that someday there would be bluebirds over the white cliffs of Dover and urging parted lovers not to sit under the apple tree "with anyone else but me," could finally anticipate the happy ending. "It's Been a Long, Long Time" captured the mood of relief and release, the almost giddy sense of joy that swept the country, as first the war in Europe moved relentlessly to an end, and then, within four months, the war in the Pacific came to an abrupt halt. The song echoed the sentiments of parents, sweethearts and returning servicemen throughout the re-awakening world.

Words by Sammy Cahn
Music by Jule Styne

Copyright © 1945 Morley Music Co. Copyright © renewed 1973 Morley Music Co. International Copyright secured. All rights reserved. Used by permission.

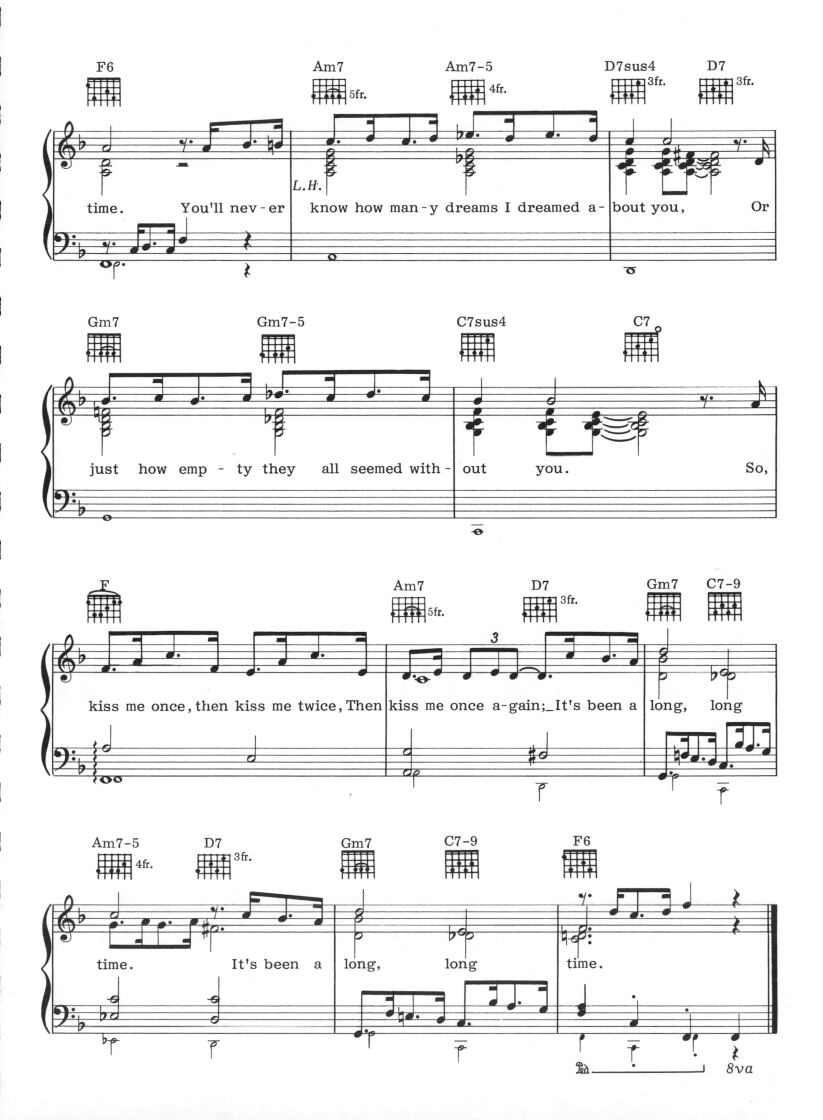

LINDA

Words and Music by Jack Lawrence

Lee V. Eastman, an attorney, music publisher and famous art collector, had a problem back in 1946. There was a song for his wife, Louise, and his children Louise, Jr., Laura and John. But there was no song for his daughter Linda. Finally, after some persuasion, his client Jack Lawrence, who also wrote "Sleepy Lagoon" and "If I Didn't Care," wrote one for her. "Linda" was recorded in 1947 by crooner Buddy Clark and became one of the top sellers of the year. It also boosted the Buddy Clark fan club membership and became the namesake for countless postwar baby girls. Today, Linda Eastman is better known as Mrs. Paul McCartney.

Copyright © 1946 John L., Linda L., Laura L., and Louise L. Eastman, Jr. Copyright © renewed 1974 MPL Communications, Inc. International Copyright secured. All rights reserved. Used by permission.

151

I Don't Want to Set the World on Fire

**Words and Music by Eddie Seiler, Sol Marcus,
Bennie Benjamin and Eddie Durham**

*Bennie Benjamin, one of the four writers of "I Don't Want to Set the World on Fire,"
conceived of the song as a lively up-tempo number when it was written in 1940. At about
the same time, Harlan Leonard's Kansas City Rockets seemed to be filling the void left
by Count Basie after the Basie band departed the green plains around Kansas City for the
greener pastures of New York. The Rockets recorded the song in 1940, giving it all
their customary exuberance, but both the record and the song flopped. For a while it
seemed that this musical spitfire would go nowhere. Then The Ink Spots came into the
picture. First, they slowed down the tempo. Next, they recorded it in 1941, employing their
magical style and gentle, laid-back touch. Much to Bennie Benjamin's surprise—pleasant
surprise, that is —the ballad tempo hit the nail on the head, and the song became a
classic. Another Benjamin hit of this period was "When the Lights Go On Again (All
Over the World)." He later teamed up with George David Weiss to form one of the hottest
collaborations of the late '40s, producing such winners as "Rumors Are Flying"
and "I Don't See Me in Your Eyes Anymore."*

Copyright © 1941 Cherio Corporation. Copyright © renewed 1969 Cherio Corporation. International Copyright secured. All rights reserved.

Love Letters

Words by Edward Heyman; Music by Victor Young

Written for the 1945 picture Love Letters, *starring Joseph Cotten and Jennifer Jones, this song had to wait 17 years before it became a real hit. Then the miracle was performed by a young and virtually unknown singer, Ketty Lester, who had been making a quick climb from San Francisco's Purple Onion nightclub to stardom in a New York revival of* Cabin in the Sky. *Her recording of "Love Letters" became a million-seller. Among Victor Young's other song triumphs are "Sweet Sue—Just You," "Stella by Starlight," "My Foolish Heart" and the wistful "Around the World," which was the theme for the Mike Todd cinematic extravaganza* Around the World in 80 Days.

Smaller hands may omit this note.

Copyright © 1945, renewed 1972 Famous Music Corporation.
This arrangement Copyright © 1982 Famous Music Corporation.

I'll Never Smile Again

Quite a few of the great popular hits owe their existence to true-life experiences—some happy, some not. Ruth Lowe, the pianist in Ina Ray Hutton's all-girl band, lost her husband while in Chicago in 1939. They had been married only a short time before. Grief-stricken, she returned to her native Toronto where, as a tribute to him and to the happiness they had shared, she wrote this, her first song. Percy Faith, who had a radio orchestra in Canada, introduced it later that year. In 1940, a young Frank Sinatra

joined Tommy Dorsey's orchestra right after making his big-band debut with Harry James' new band about a year earlier. Within a few months, he had made his mark in the pop music world with his performance of "I'll Never Smile Again," and the record made an indelible impression on everyone who heard it. Though it was composer Lowe's only hit, it was, thanks to Sinatra and Dorsey, a resounding one.

Words and Music by Ruth Lowe

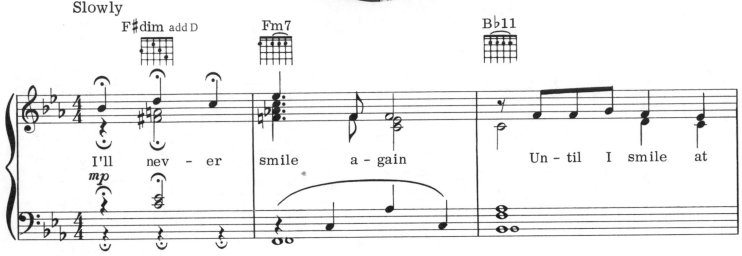

I'll nev-er smile a-gain Un-til I smile at you. I'll nev-er laugh a-gain; What good would it do? For

Copyright © 1939 MCA Music, a division of MCA Inc., New York, N.Y. Copyright renewed. International Copyright secured. All rights reserved. Used by permission.

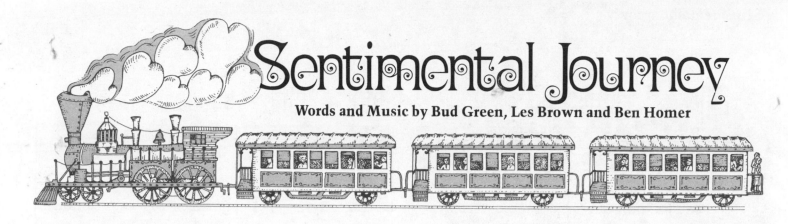

Sentimental Journey

Words and Music by Bud Green, Les Brown and Ben Homer

It took a generous music publisher, an arranger who needed some money, a bandleader with big ideas and a girl singer who was willing to stretch her voice to bring "Sentimental Journey" to successful fruition. Ben Homer, the arranger for Les Brown's band during World War II, was the one in need of money. Buddy Morris was the publisher who offered him an advance and a place to work. Les Brown was the bandleader who worked with Homer on the tune and who, in his own words, "made the song too rangy"—that is, covering such a wide range that it was difficult for most singers. Doris Day, the band's vocalist, had the range to cope with Brown's expansive ideas. "Sentimental Journey" became such a smash hit for Les Brown that he started using it as his signature theme.

Copyright © 1944 Morley Music Co. Copyright © renewed 1972 Morley Music Co.
International Copyright secured. All rights reserved. Used by permission.

Words and Music by
Joan Whitney and Alex Kramer

From their 12th-floor studio overlooking New York City's harbor, native Montrealer Alex Kramer and his American wife Joan Whitney would see ships arrive and depart each day. One afternoon in 1948, while struggling for a song idea, they watched as a beautiful passenger liner slowly moved out of its berth. "Where do you think that ship is heading?" they asked—and they had their song. In 1949, "Far Away Places" made the No. 1 spot on the Hit Parade and stayed on the show for 19 straight weeks, and the recording by Bing Crosby and The Ken Darby Choir was a best-seller. The song also achieved the notable success of selling a million sheet-music copies.

Moderately slow

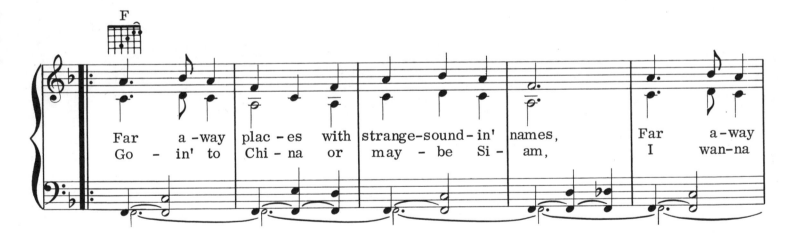

Far a-way plac-es with strange-sound-in' names,
Go - in' to Chi - na or may - be Si - am,

Far a-way I wan-na

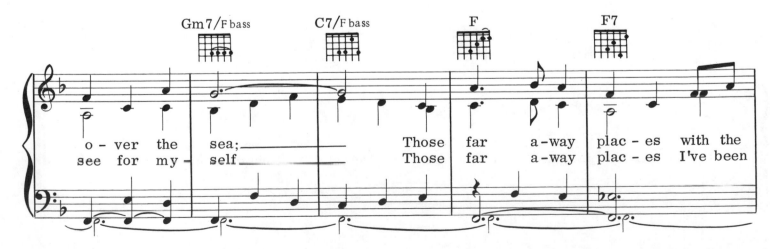

o - ver the sea; Those far a-way plac-es with the
see for my-self Those far a-way plac-es I've been

Copyright © 1948 Bourne Co. Copyright renewed. This arrangement Copyright © 1982 Bourne Co.

Tangerine

Words by Johnny Mercer; Music by Victor Schertzinger

Though Victor Schertzinger was best known as a motion picture director in the 1920s and '30s, he originally was a violinist and conductor, and composed music all through his directing career. Two of his best-known songs were the glowingly romantic ballads "Marcheta" and "One Night of Love." "Tangerine," with lyrics by Johnny Mercer, was also a heartthrobber until Bob Eberly and Helen O'Connell sang it with Jimmy Dorsey's orchestra in the 1942 film The Fleet's In *and gave it the same slow-fast-slow swinging treatment that they applied to such other Dorsey hits as "Green Eyes" and "Amapola."*

Copyright © 1942, renewed 1969 Famous Music Corporation. This arrangement Copyright © 1982 Famous Music Corporation.

Tangerine

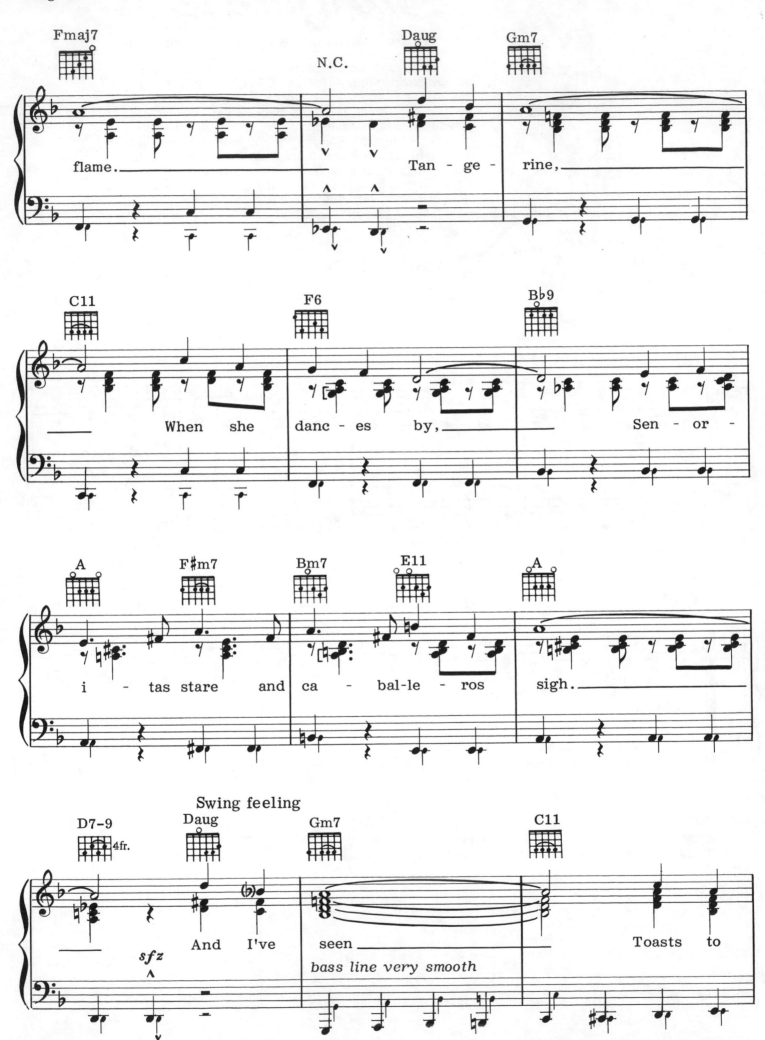

Seems Like Old Times

Words and Music by Carmen Lombardo and John Jacob Loeb

The year was 1946, and World War II had finally come to an end. All over the country, people began to feel relief and nostalgia for the good old times they'd left behind. Carmen Lombardo and John Jacob Loeb were working on a lively song with a sarcastic attitude about getting the runaround: "You're still fooling around with somebody else—seems like old times." Guy Lombardo told them they were getting the wrong feeling. "They were trying to rewrite 'Goody-Goody,'" he later recalled.

He shifted some of the lyrics, removed the sarcasm and slowed down the tempo. It was the only song that Guy had ever helped write (although he took no credit for his work), and it was an overnight smash. Arthur Godfrey heard the song a few days after the record was released and started playing it so often on his radio show that it became his theme. More than three decades later, "Seems Like Old Times" was revived by Woody Allen for his 1977 Oscar-winning film Annie Hall.

Copyright © 1946, renewed 1973 Ahlert-Burke Corp.
for U.S.A. Rights outside the U.S.A. controlled by Leo Feist, Inc.

The Nearness of You

Words by Ned Washington; Music by Hoagy Carmichael

Very few popular songs have been successfully introduced by opera stars on the screen. Gladys Swarthout, however, was no ordinary opera star during her heyday in the 1930s. She looked like a movie star and had a voice that could encompass the range of a pop song without sounding pretentious. Between 1936 and 1939, she made five films, playing a straight dramatic role in the last one. "The Nearness of You" was her final song in films and was featured in the 1938 motion picture Romance in the Dark, *in which she starred with John Boles and John Barrymore. Hoagy Carmichael, who composed "The Nearness of You," counts it among his four favorite of his own compositions (the others are "Stardust," "Rockin' Chair" and "One Morning in May"). In 1940, Glenn Miller and his band recorded the song with Ray Eberle doing the vocal honors, and it was this version that contributed so much to its ultimate popularity.*

Copyright © 1937 and 1940, renewed 1964 and 1967 Famous Music Corporation. This arrangement Copyright © 1982 Famous Music Corporation.

Daddy's Little Girl

Words and Music by
Bobby Burke and Horace Gerlach

A Boston disc jockey brought this sentimental song to the attention of The Mills Brothers in 1949. Donald Mills, who had a little girl of his own—and who usually discovered the group's hits—fell in love with it, as did his brothers and their father. Today, it is a wedding tradition to play "Daddy's Little Girl" when the bride dances with her father.

You're the end of the rain-bow, My pot o' gold; You're Dad-dy's lit-tle girl To have and hold. A pre-cious gem is what you are; You're Mom-my's bright and shin - ing

176

Copyright © 1949 Cherio Corporation. Copyright © renewed 1977 Cherio Corporation. International Copyright secured. All rights reserved.

While We're Young

Words by Bill Engvick; Music by Alec Wilder and Morty Palitz

Alec Wilder, who died in 1980, started his career as a novelist, but after writing a manuscript three feet high, he discovered that he "didn't have anything to write about." Next, the would-be author tried music, then experimental film, then poetry, before finally returning to music as a serious composer. He wrote symphonic works, music for children, jazz-oriented humorous pieces such as "The Neurotic Goldfish," "It's Silk, Feel It" and "Jack, This Is My Husband." Wilder also composed some of America's finest popular tunes, including "It's So Peaceful in the Country" and "While We're Young," first sung by the legendary Mabel Mercer in 1943.

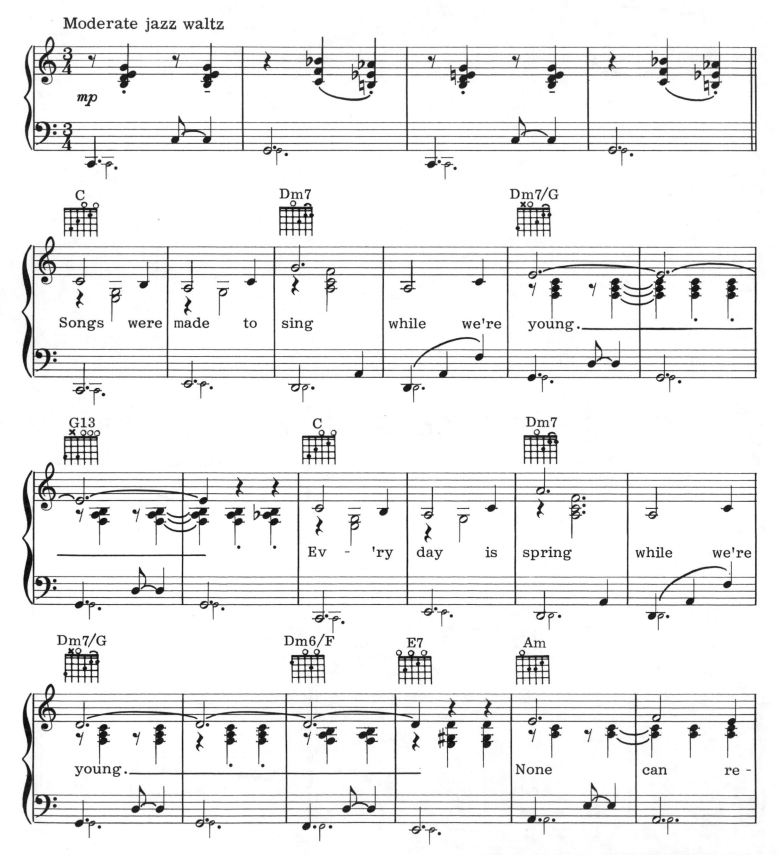

TRO — Copyright © 1943 (renewed 1971) and 1944 (renewed 1972) Ludlow Music, Inc., New York, N.Y. International Copyright secured. All rights reserved. Used by permission.

HITS PLAYED ROUND THE WORLD

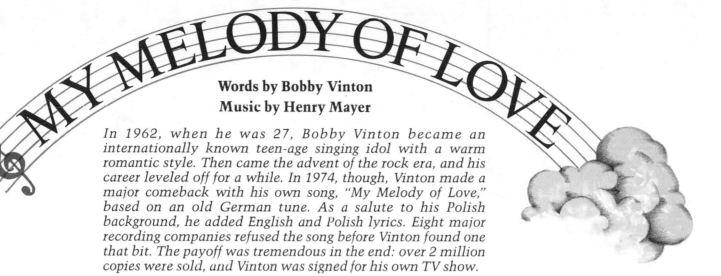

MY MELODY OF LOVE

Words by Bobby Vinton
Music by Henry Mayer

In 1962, when he was 27, Bobby Vinton became an internationally known teen-age singing idol with a warm romantic style. Then came the advent of the rock era, and his career leveled off for a while. In 1974, though, Vinton made a major comeback with his own song, "My Melody of Love," based on an old German tune. As a salute to his Polish background, he added English and Polish lyrics. Eight major recording companies refused the song before Vinton found one that bit. The payoff was tremendous in the end: over 2 million copies were sold, and Vinton was signed for his own TV show.

Moderate polka, in 2 (♩ = 1 beat)

look - ing for a place to go So I can be all a - lone
wish I had a place to hide All my sor - row, all my pride.

From thoughts and mem-o - ries,___ So that when the
I just can't get a - long,___ 'Cause the love

Copyright © 1973, 1974 Edition Rhythmus Rolf Budde KG, Berlin, Germany, and Radio Music International, Luxembourg. All rights for U.S.A. controlled by Pedro Music Corp., Los Angeles, California. All rights for Canada controlled by Morning Music Ltd., Ontario, Canada.

VOLARE

NEL BLU, DIPINTO DI BLU

English words by Mitchell Parish; Italian words by Domenico Modugno and F. Migliacci; Music by Domenico Modugno

Written by Sicilian gypsy Domenico Modugno, who claims descent from gypsy royalty, this song first appeared as "Nel Blu, Dipinto di Blu" in 1958, winning first prize at the Italian San Remo Song Festival as well as a Grammy in the U.S.A. several months later. In 1960, Bobby Rydell recorded a version with English lyrics by Mitchell Parish and made it a hit all over again. Since then, its carefree swing has kept it popular with singers and audiences alike.

Some - times the world is a val - ley of heart-aches and tears,
Pen - so che un so - gno co - sì non ri - tor - ni mai più,

And in the hus - tle and bus - tle, no sun-shine ap - pears,
Mi di-pin-ge-vo le ma - ni e la fac - cia di blu,

But you and I have our love al - ways there to re - mind us
Poi d'im-prov-vi-so ve - ni - vo dal ven - to ra - pi - to

Copyright © 1958 Edizioni Curci. Rights for the U.S.A., its territories and possessions, and Canada controlled by Robbins Music Corporation.

There is a way we can leave all the shad-ows be-hind us.
E in-co-min-cia-vo a vo- la - re nel cie-lo in-fi- ni - to.
slower

Moderately, with a lilt

Vo - la - re,_____ oh, oh!_____ Can -
Vo - la - re,_____ oh, oh!_____ Can -

ta - re,_____ oh, oh, oh, oh!_____ Let's
ta - re,_____ oh, oh, oh, oh!_____ Nel

fly way up in the clouds, A- way from the mad-d'n-ing crowds. We can
blu, di-pin-to di blu, Fe- li- ce di sta-re las- sù, E vo-

Volare

186

The River Seine
(La Seine)

English words by Allan Roberts and Alan Holt
French words by Flavien Monod and Guy LaFarge
Music by Guy LaFarge

What "Vienna, My City of Dreams" is to the Austrian capital, what "Arrivederci, Roma" is to Rome, so "The River Seine" is to Paris: the glorious anthem of a glorious city. It began as "La Seine," written in 1948 by French composer Guy LaFarge. Five years later, with new English lyrics, "The River Seine" became one of Guy Lombardo's standards. When you listen to it, you can almost hear the accordions and taxicabs outside a small Paris café.

Freely

When-

ev – er it's spring-time in Pa – ris ___ And man-y hearts are a lon
La Seine est a – ven-tu – reu – se ___ De Châ-til- lon à Mé-

flame, ___ I wan-der down to the riv – er,
ry, ___ Et son hu- meur voy-a- geu-se,

188

Copyright © 1945 Royalty, Éditions Musicales, Paris, France. Copyright renewed 1953 Warner Bros. Inc. All rights reserved.

The River Seine

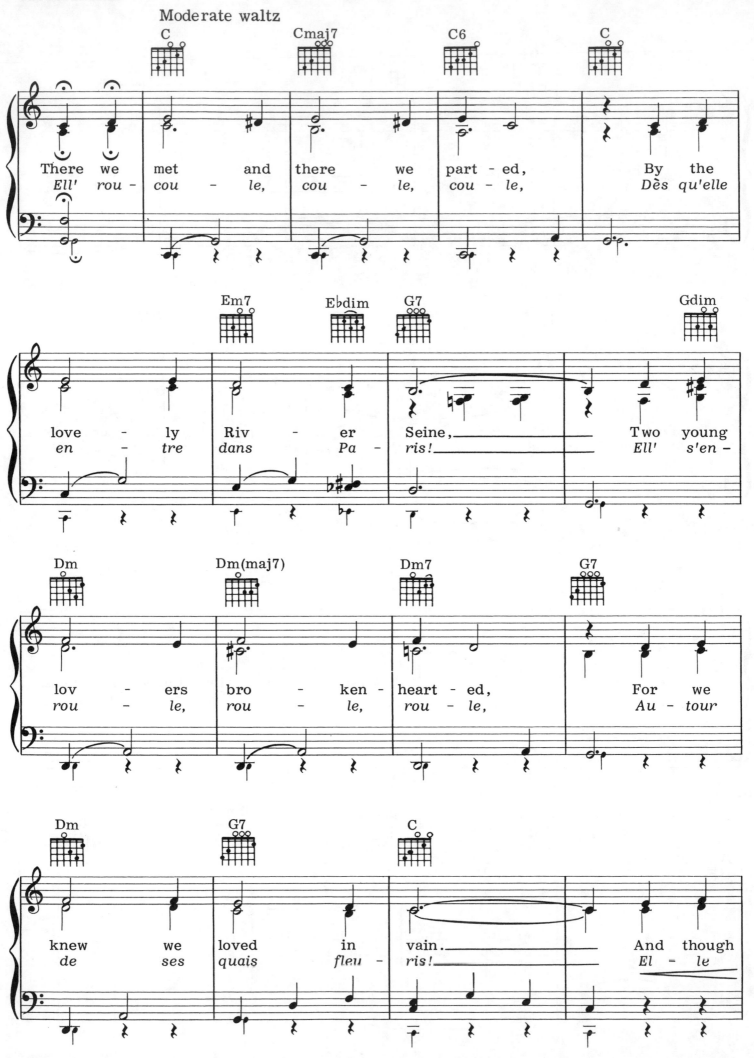

Beyond the Sea
(La Mer)

French words and Music by Charles Trenet
English words by Jack Lawrence

During the '30s and '40s, Charles Trenet, probably France's most popular singer and entertainer next to Maurice Chevalier, was also the most prolific of French songwriters. His surging "La Mer," written in 1945, contains many Debussy-like suggestions of Impressionism. Jack Lawrence (of "Linda" and "Tenderly" fame) wrote English lyrics for it in 1947, and in 1960, Bobby Darin's recording of "Beyond the Sea" became a million-seller.

Copyright © 1945 and 1946, renewed 1973 Éditions Raoul Breton. Copyright © 1947 T. B. Harms Company. Copyright renewed 1975 MPL Communications, Inc.
This arrangement Copyright © 1982 T. B. Harms Company. International Copyright secured. All rights reserved. Used by permission.

Beyond the Sea

PERFIDIA

English words by Milton Leeds
Spanish words and Music by Alberto Dominguez

In 1940, disc jockeys looked to Latin America for songs they could broadcast, due to a battle between the radio broadcasters and the American Society of Composers, Authors and Publishers (ASCAP) that kept almost all American songs off the air. One of their first finds was the haunting "Perfidia," by the Mexican Alberto Dominguez. Though Xavier Cugat promoted the song here in 1939, it was Glenn Miller's 1941 version that really launched it. Other recordings soon followed by Benny Goodman, Jimmy Dorsey, The Mills Brothers and Tony Martin.

Copyright © 1939 and 1941 Peer International Corporation. Copyright renewed. Used by permission.

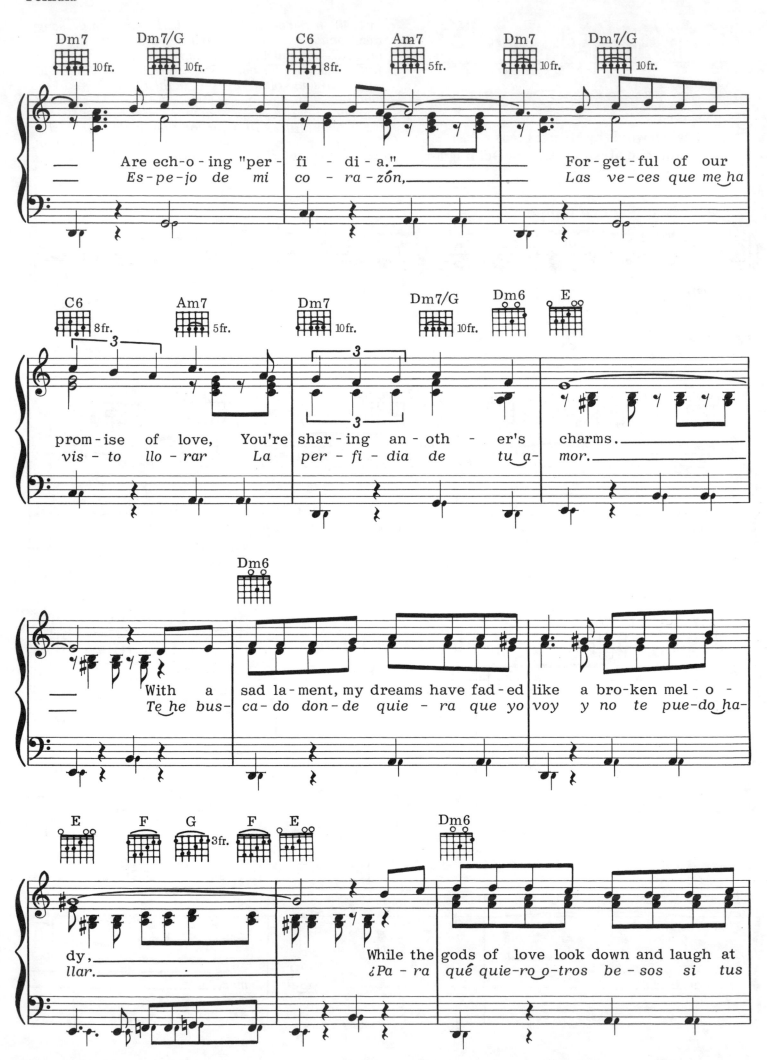

Bésame Mucho

English words by Sunny Skylar
Spanish words and Music by Consuelo Velazquez

Consuelo Velazquez is one of Mexico's two famous women songwriters (her distinguished colleague being Maria Grever). A concert pianist as well as a popular artist, she wrote "Bésame Mucho" ("Kiss Me Much") in 1941, and it first reached American audiences through Jimmy Dorsey's 1944 hit recording featuring vocals by Kitty Kallen and Bob Eberly, with English lyrics by Sunny Skylar. That disc sold well over a million copies, but a test recording by the young Andy Russell, released that same year, was a big surprise. Andy's bilingual version, sung in his warm and intimate style, made it a jukebox winner and started him on a successful career.

Bé - sa - me,_____ bé - sa - me mu - cho,_____
Bé - sa - me,_____ bé - sa - me mu - cho,_____

Each time I cling to your kiss, I hear music di -
Co - mo si fue - ra es - ta no - che la úl - ti - ma

Copyright © 1941 and 1943 Promotora Hispano Americana de Musica S.A. Copyrights renewed.
Sole Selling Agent: Peer International Corporation. Used by permission.

Song of the Islands
NA LEI O HAWAII
Words and Music by Charles E. King

Charles E. King, Hawaii's first internationally known composer, was born on the estate of Queen Emma Kaleleonalani in 1874. Orphaned at an early age, he was adopted by his mother's family and taken under the wing of good Queen Emma, who encouraged him to study music. King later became a prominent music educator and conductor, as well as a composer, arranger and collector of over 200 Hawaiian songs. His "Song of the Islands," the quintessential melody of the South Pacific, was composed in 1915 and became the best known and best loved of all his works. If you really want to hit in Honolulu, sing it in the original Hawaiian.

Copyright © 1982 Edward B. Marks Music Corporation. All rights reserved. Used by permission.

*small notes for Hawaiian lyric only; do not play.

Waltzing Matilda

Words by A. B. (Banjo) Paterson
Music by Marie Cowan

On a visit to Queensland in his native Australia in 1895, poet "Banjo" Paterson heard a rancher say that he had seen two men "waltzing Matilda down by the billabong" —meaning that he had seen the men carrying their swags (bedrolls) by a water hole. Inspired by the colorful slang of the Outback, Paterson wrote what became Down Under's best-known and best-loved song. It tells of a swagman (drifter) caught stealing a jumbuck (sheep) from a squatter (rancher). Swagmen, for those who don't speak "Australian," boil water in a "billy" and carry food in a "tucker-bag." Informally, "Matilda" is Australia's national song.

Copyright © 1936 Allan & Co. Prop. Ltd., Melbourne, Australia. Copyright © 1941 Carl Fischer, Inc., New York, N.Y.
This arrangement Copyright © 1982 Carl Fischer, Inc. International Copyright secured. All rights reserved.

205

Vienna, My City of Dreams
WIEN, DU STADT MEINER TRÄUME

English words by Kim Gannon
German words and Music by Rudolf Sieczynski

*Perhaps even more than Johann Strauss's "Blue Danube," this lovely
waltz is, to modern listeners at least, the song most evocative
of Vienna. Composed by a Viennese music teacher named Rudolf
Sieczynski (1879-1952), it was published as Opus 1 in 1914,
on the eve of the war that was to destroy the Hapsburg
Empire. Gratifyingly, it was an immediate hit, but it
proved to be Sieczynski's only one. Nevertheless, it
became the virtual theme song of the Austrian
tenor Richard Tauber, who sang it so often that
many persons believed he had composed it. Of
the several English versions, this one comes
closest to the spirit of the original.*

Copyright © 1914 Adolf Robitschek. Copyright © 1940 Warner Bros. Inc. Copyrights
renewed. All rights for the United States and Canada controlled by Warner Bros. Inc. All rights reserved.

thrill of the dance, Live on like a love-ly re-frain._____ The
bin ich halt z'haus Bei Tag und noch mehr bei der Nacht,_____ Und

thou-sand de-lights of mag-i-cal nights I spent in your star-light that
kei-ner bleibt kalt, ob jung o-der alt, Der Wein, wie es wirk-lich ist

gleams._____ I'm liv-ing till when I'm with you a-gain, Vi-
kennt._____ Müsst ein-mal ich fort von dem schö-nen Ort, Da

en-na, my cit-y of dreams._____ Your song ling-ers
nehm' mei-ne Sehn-sucht kein End'._____ Dann hört ich aus

SECTION 8
Pages 210–218
OPERETTA GEMS

Words by Henry Blossom
Music by Victor Herbert

from "Mlle. Modiste"

One of the most purely sensuous of Victor Herbert's melodies, "Kiss Me Again" was originally the final section of an extended parody scene in his 1905 operetta Mlle. Modiste. Fifi, the leading character, dreams of becoming an actress and demonstrates her dramatic gifts by performing a country maid's gavotte, a noblewoman's polonaise and finally this dreamy and emotional waltz. After his leading lady, the vivacious Fritzi Scheff, kept stopping the show with it night after night, Herbert decided to extract "Kiss Me Again," flesh it out a bit and let it shine on its own. It was a stroke of genius: the song became Fritzi Scheff's theme till the end of her career, and "Kiss Me Again" has now been shining brilliantly for three quarters of a century.

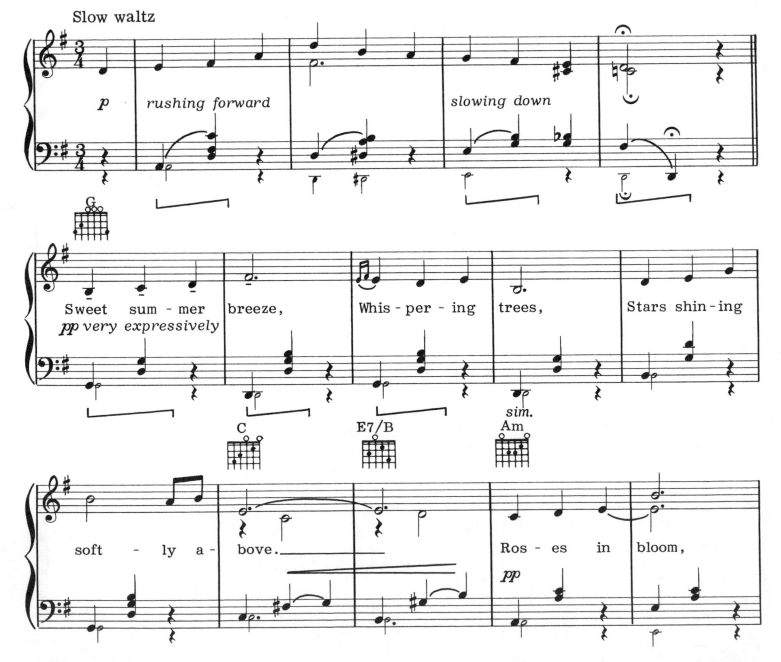

Copyright © 1915 Warner Bros. Inc. Copyright renewed. All rights reserved.

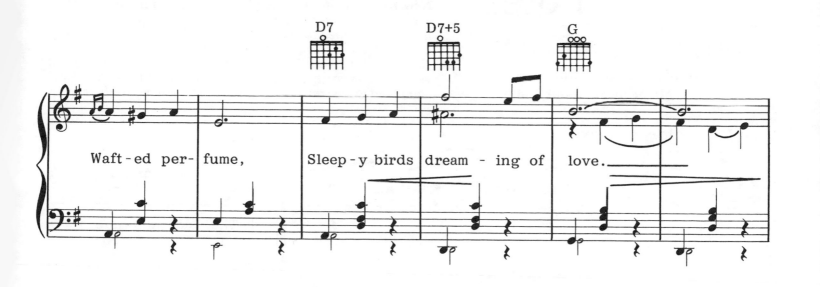

Waft-ed per-fume, Sleep-y birds dream-ing of love.

Safe in your arms, Far from a-larms, Day-light shall

come but in vain. *cresc.* Ten-der-ly pressed

Close to your breast, Kiss me, Kiss me a-gain.

from "The New Moon"

Lover, Come Back to Me

Words by Oscar Hammerstein II
Music by Sigmund Romberg

Although The New Moon was a box-office smash once it got to New York in 1928, the operetta nearly folded in Philadelphia. Tryouts there were received so badly that Romberg and his librettists decided to close the show and rewrite it completely. Luckily they succeeded by adding such numbers as "Lover, Come Back to Me," one of the most poignant expressions of yearning ever written. The song, with its climactic melody, was composed for the musical's prima donna, Evelyn Herbert.

Copyright © 1928 Warner Bros. Inc. Copyright renewed. All rights reserved.

213

ROSE-MARIE

from "Rose-Marie"

Words by Otto Harbach and Oscar Hammerstein II
Music by Rudolf Friml

Rose-Marie was planned as a stage spectacle about the winter carnival in Quebec City. Its producer wanted the show to culminate with the melting down of a giant ice palace. Told this was impractical on stage — the audience might drown — he dropped the carnival, but not the Canadian setting. Thus the Mounties went to Broadway in 1924. They went to Hollywood in 1936 with Nelson Eddy and Jeanette MacDonald, and with Howard Keel and Ann Blyth in 1954.

Rose - Ma - rie, I love you! I'm al - ways dream - ing of you. No mat - ter what I do, I can't for-get you; Some - times I wish that I had nev - er met you!

Copyright © 1924 Warner Bros. Inc. Copyright renewed. All rights reserved.

And yet if I should lose you,____ ____ 'Twould

mean my ver - y life to me.____ Of

all the queens that ev - er lived, I'd choose you____ To

rule me, my Rose - Ma - rie.

It is hard to imagine Franz Lehár's operetta The Merry Widow as daring or revolutionary, but in the Vienna of 1905 there were those who were shocked by the sensuous qualities of the score. "This isn't music!" a director of the Theater an der Wien is said to have exclaimed. What he thought it was we'll never know. But regardless, the Widow — and her delicious waltz — triumphed then and have continued ever since to charm and excite lis-

MERRY WIDOW WALTZ

from "The Merry Widow"
Music by Franz Lehár, adapted by Dan Fox

teners throughout the world. So popular was the operetta and so great was audience demand to see it that at one time in cosmopolitan Buenos Aires, The Merry Widow was playing simultaneously in five languages at five different theaters! Although the waltz is sung in the operetta, Dan Fox has made our arrangement for piano only, but he has included all three main themes of the waltz for your musical enjoyment.

Copyright © 1982 Padmi Publishing Co. for U.S.A. only. Copyright © 1932 Chappell Music Canada Ltd.

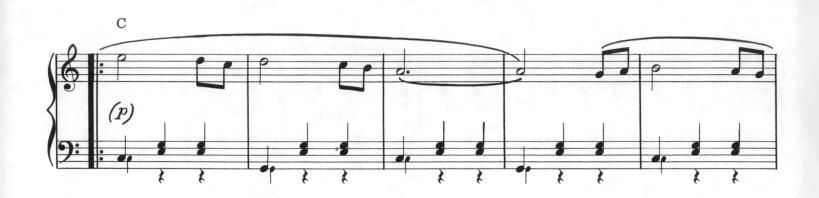

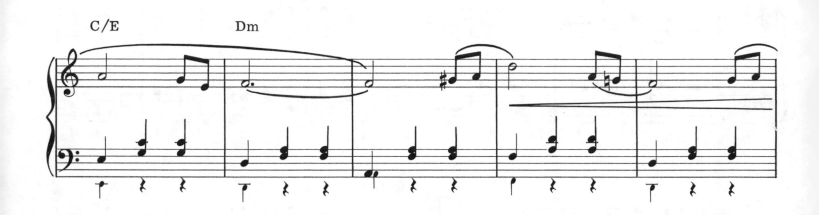

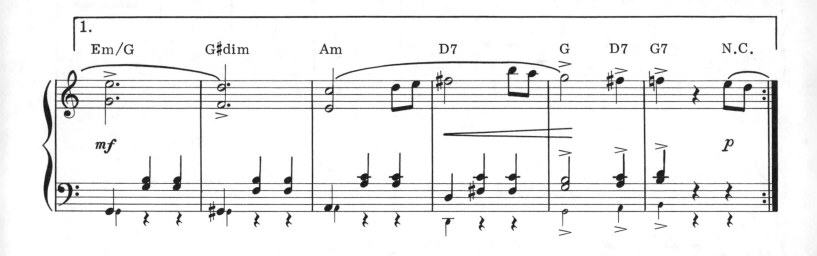

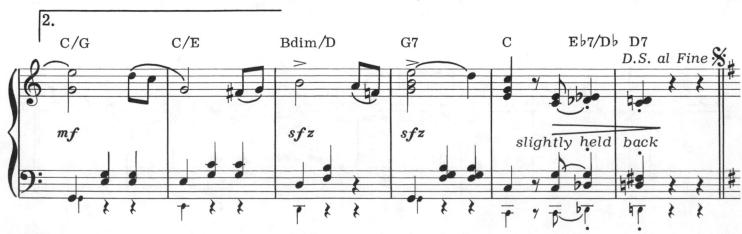

When You Were Sweet Sixteen
Words and Music by James Thornton

The favorite pianist and drinking companion of prizefighter John L. Sullivan, songwriter and vaudeville star Jim Thornton was famous up and down Broadway for the alcoholic marathons and tipsy escapades he enjoyed each night after the show. Steeped as well in Shakespeare and Irish blarney, he was married to another vaudevillian, Bonnie Thornton, who often administered the bromo while asking her wayward spouse if he still loved her. "Sure!" he replied on one occasion, "I love you as I did when you were sweet sixteen." And in the morning, along with a hangover, a million-copy song hit was born.

Slowly and somewhat freely throughout

When first I saw the love-light in your eye And heard the voice like sweet-est mel-o-dy Speak words of love to my en-rap-tured soul, The world had naught but joy in store for

Copyright © 1982 Ardee Music Publishing, Inc., for U.S.A. World rights, except for U.S.A., Shapiro, Bernstein & Co. Inc., New York, N.Y.

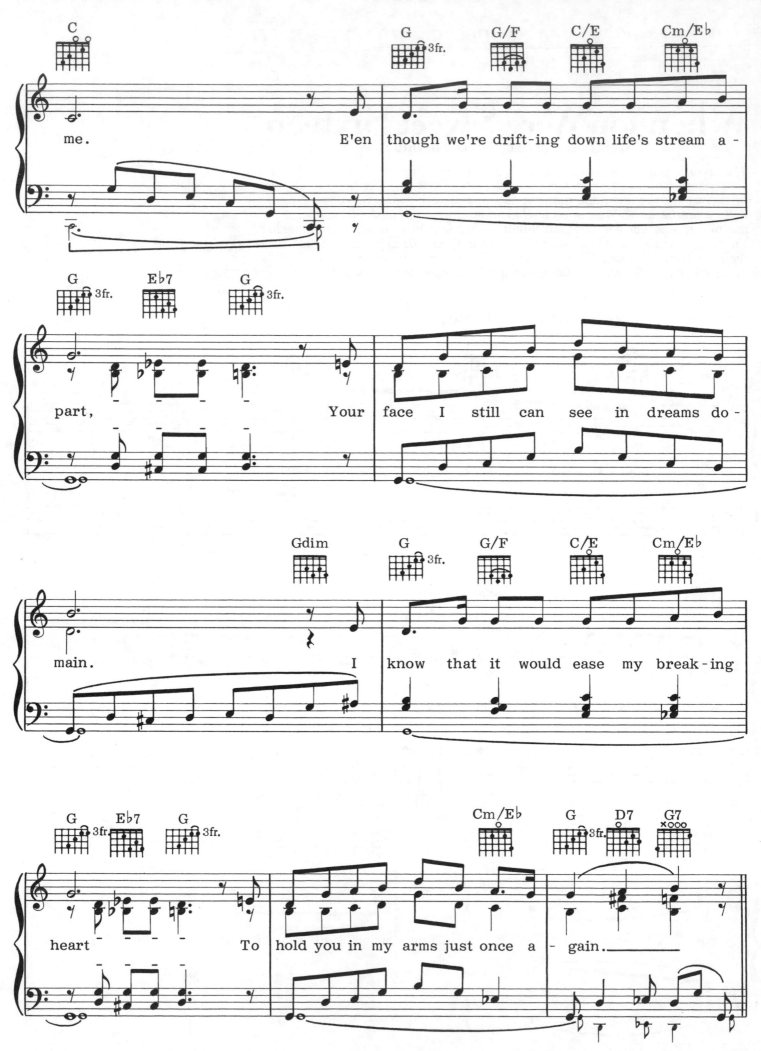

Take Me Out to the Ball Game

Words by Jack Norworth; Music by Albert Von Tilzer

According to the apocryphal chronicles of popular music, neither composer nor lyricist had ever seen a baseball game when the two men sat down in 1908 to write what was to become the anthem of our national sport. In fact, the story has it that 20 years elapsed before either man spent an afternoon at the diamond. Albert Von Tilzer's successful introduction of this number on the stage led to a contract to tour the Orpheum vaudeville circuit, while Jack Norworth and his wife, Nora Bayes, helped to popularize the song even further. It has been used since in virtually every motion picture about the game, and today, Norworth's first draft of the lyrics is in the Baseball Hall of Fame at Cooperstown, New York.

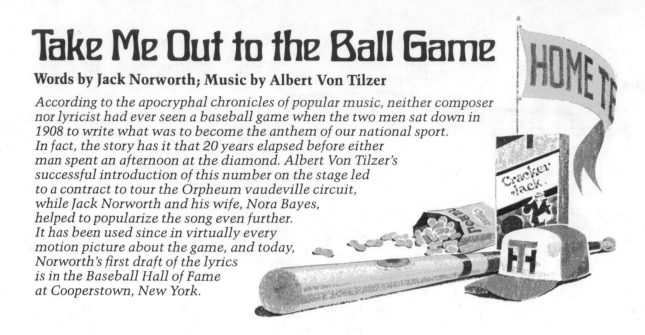

In a rollicking 3

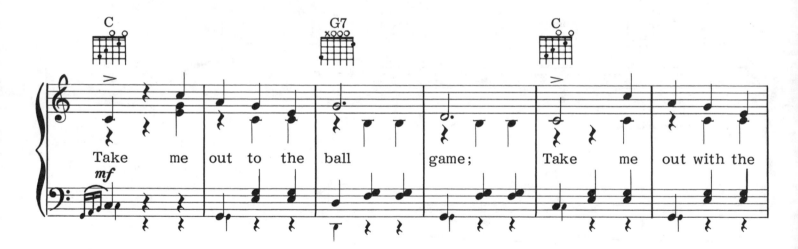

Take me out to the ball game; Take me out with the

crowd.___ Buy me some pea-nuts and Crack - er Jack;

Copyright © 1908, renewed 1936 and assigned to Jerry Vogel Music Co., Inc., and Broadway Music Corporation.

My Melancholy Baby

Words by George Norton; Music by Ernie Burnett

Like "Three O'Clock in the Morning," this tuneful song has become a classic expression of an end-of-the-evening feeling. Unfortunately, it has had a long association with drunkards and saloon pianists, which is a shame, since it's really quite a beauty. Originally called "Melancholy," it was first heard around 1912 at the Dutch Mill in Denver, Colorado, then one of the more elegant spots in the West, and it went on to become a popular vaudeville number. Its red-eyed reputation was acquired during the late '20s, when it was frequently featured by Tommy Lyman, a cabaret singer whose habit was to begin work at midnight and continue to perform into the wee hours or until he was ready to pass out from sheer exhaustion.

Come sweet-heart mine,___ Don't sit and pine,___
Birds in the trees,___ Whis-per-ing breeze,___

Tell me of the cares that make you feel so blue. What have I done?___
Should not fail to lull you in-to peace-ful dreams. So, tell me why___

An-swer me, hon';___ Have I ev-er said an un-kind word to you?
Sad-ly you sigh,___ Sit-ting at the win-dow where the pale moon beams.

Copyright © 1911, renewed 1938 and assigned to Shapiro, Bernstein & Co. Inc. and Jerry Vogel Music Co., Inc.

SHINE ON, HARVEST MOON

Words and Music by Nora Bayes and Jack Norworth

"Shine On, Harvest Moon," probably the song most often sung by folks sitting around the fireside, was written by the vaudeville team of Nora Bayes and her husband, Jack Norworth, in 1908. Later that year, the highly temperamental Miss Bayes interpolated the song in the Ziegfeld Follies, and it remained closely linked to her for the rest of her career. Ironically, although they insisted upon being billed as "The Stage's Happiest Couple," Mr. and Mrs. Norworth didn't remain happy for long and were divorced in 1913. According to Edgar Leslie, the last line of "Shine On, Harvest Moon" gave him the idea for his own famous song "For Me and My Gal."

With a lilt; not too fast

Oh, shine on, shine on, har-vest moon____ Up in the sky. I ain't had no lov - in' since

Copyright © 1908 Warner Bros. Inc., renewed and assigned to Warner Bros. Inc. and Jerry Vogel Music Company, Inc. Published by Warner Bros. Inc. and Jerry Vogel Music Company, Inc., in the U.S.A. This arrangement Copyright © 1982 Warner Bros. Inc. and Jerry Vogel Music Company, Inc. All rights reserved.

January, February, June or July. Snow time
ain't no time to stay Out-doors and spoon. So,
shine on, shine on, har-vest moon, For me and my

1. gal. Oh,

2. gal.

229

The Darktown Strutters' Ball

Words and Music by Shelton Brooks

Like many a Canadian musician of his day, black composer-lyricist Shelton Brooks left his native Amherstburg, Ontario, to pursue a career in the U.S.A. His two biggest hits were "Some of These Days," written in 1910, and "The Darktown Strutters' Ball," composed eight years later. Both numbers became closely identified with Sophie Tucker, whose success with the latter song was so great at Reisenweber's famous New York cabaret that the room in which she sang was renamed the Sophie Tucker Room.

Moderately

mf

I'll be down to get you in a tax - i, hon-ey, You bet-ter be read - y a-bout half-past eight.__ Now, dear - ie, don't be late;__ I want to be there when the

Copyright © 1917 (renewed 1945) Leo Feist, Inc.

After the Ball

Words and Music by Charles K. Harris

The granddaddy of all smash hits, "After the Ball" failed at its premiere in 1892 because the singer forgot the words. Even so, Milwaukeean Charles K. Harris paid to have his song interpolated in the show A Trip to Chinatown. Though it bore no relation to the plot, it brought down the house. Soon a Boston music shop ordered 75,000 copies, and by year's end, Harris was using every available printing press in Milwaukee to satisfy the demand. Within a few years, 5 million copies had been sold, and in later life, Harris claimed to have made $10 million from the song.

Moderate waltz

Af-ter the ball is o - ver, Af-ter the break of morn,_____ Af-ter the danc-ers' leav - ing,

Copyright © 1982 Padmi Publishing Co.

Ballin' the Jack

Words by Jim Burris; Music by Chris Smith

One of the first of a long line of "dance instruction" numbers, this great favorite was written way back in 1913, at the time when Vernon and Irene Castle were popularizing such zoological ballroom novelties as the camel walk, the grizzly bear, the turkey trot and the more lasting fox-trot. A Dixieland toe-tapper during the '20s and '30s, "Ballin' the Jack" was used in three films (For Me and My Gal, On the Riviera and That's My Boy) and has been a staple of Danny Kaye's repertoire. Chubby Checkers even made it a twist hit during the '60s. The title comes from railroad slang: "jack," a Negro folk term for "locomotive" (based on the legendary toughness of the jackass), and "highball," the trainman's signal to start rolling. Thus, "ballin' the jack" simply means traveling fast while enjoying a good time.

First you put your two knees close up tight,—Then you sway 'em to the left, Then you

sway 'em to the right. Step a-round the floor kind of nice and light,—Then you

Copyright © 1982 Edward B. Marks Music Corporation. All rights reserved. Used by permission.

AFTER YOU'VE GONE

Words and Music by Henry Creamer and Turner Layton

This song, written by the black vaudeville team of Creamer and Layton, who also created "Way Down Yonder in New Orleans," became a standard almost before the ink was dry. Al Jolson introduced it at New York's Winter Garden in 1918, and both Sophie Tucker and Louis Armstrong included it in their repertoires during the '20s. It became a Benny Goodman jazz classic in 1935 (he was to record it again many times), a Bing Crosby winner when he recorded it with the Paul Whiteman band, a Judy Garland favorite in the 1942 film For Me and My Gal, and it even gave Shirley MacLaine a chance to show her many talents in the 1958 film Some Came Running. Though the song has been around for quite some time, the torch is still burning brightly.

Copyright © 1918 Morley Music Co. Copyright © renewed 1946 Morley Music Co.
International Copyright secured. All rights reserved. Used by permission.

MARY'S A GRAND OLD NAME

Words and Music by George M. Cohan

This grand old song comes from George M. Cohan's musical comedy Forty-Five Minutes from Broadway, *which opened on Broadway in 1906. The characters in the story, which was set in New Rochelle, a suburb north of New York City, included a chronic gambler and horseplayer, Kid Burns, and a housemaid with an inheritance, Mary Jane. Victor Moore, on his way to becoming one of Broadway's greatest comedians, played Burns, while opposite him was the vaudeville star Fay Templeton, making her musical comedy debut as the maid. When she introduced herself by singing "Mary's a Grand Old Name," the house came down, and an immortal tune was born. In 1942, the song achieved renewed popularity when it was featured in the Cohan film biography* Yankee Doodle Dandy, *starring another immortal—James Cagney.*

Copyright © 1982 Ardee Music Publishing, Inc., for U.S.A. World rights, except for U.S.A., George M. Cohan Music Publishing Co., Inc.

School Days

Words by Will D. Cobb; Music by Gus Edwards

Gus Edwards is a sterling example of just what an immigrant can make of himself in the U.S.A. with a lot of talent and a little pluck. Born in Germany, he came here as a boy, first working in a cigar store, then plugging songs in Bowery pleasure gardens. In 1896, he went into vaudeville as part of a juvenile act. While entertaining troops during the Spanish-American War, he met Will Cobb, who became his collaborator on

such songs as "I Can't Tell Why I Love You But I Do" (revived in the 1944 film *The Belle of the Yukon*) and others. With Vincent Bryan, he wrote the famous "In My Merry Oldsmobile" in 1905, and two years later, with Cobb again, he wrote his most outstanding success, "School Days," which sold over 3,000,000 copies of sheet music. Another Edwards hit is "By the Light of the Silvery Moon," which will be sung as long as there are soft shoes and straw hats.

Copyright © MCMVI and MCMVII, renewed, Shapiro, Bernstein & Co. Inc., New York, N.Y., and Mills Music Co., New York, N.Y.

I WANT A GIRL

Words by William Dillon; Music by Harry Von Tilzer

Harry Von Tilzer, whose other hits include "Wait Till the Sun Shines, Nellie," "A Bird in a Gilded Cage" and "Under the Yum Yum Tree," wrote songs during a time when sentiment was a hot commodity. Devotion to Mother was a pet theme of his, and his most successful expression of those pre-Freudian values was this great sing-along gem written in 1911. During World War II, a more cynical generation changed the title of the song to "I Want a Girl Just Like the Girl That Married Harry James" (who happened to be married at the time to Betty Grable). Incidentally, Von Tilzer, who is credited with inventing the term "Tin Pan Alley," is among the most prolific of all composers in the Songwriters' Hall of Fame. He was also one of the first songwriters to start his own publishing company, an enterprise upon which he embarked in the early 1900s.

Copyright © 1911 Harry Von Tilzer Music Pub. Co. Copyright renewed. This arrangement Copyright © 1982 Harry Von Tilzer Music Pub. Co. International Copyright secured. All rights reserved. Used by permission.

TWELFTH STREET RAG

Music by Euday L. Bowman

Euday Bowman, a peripatetic pianist from Texas, wrote this high-flying ragtime classic in 1914 to celebrate one of the main streets in Kansas City's red-light district. Though it was originally a piano solo, it received its first set of lyrics in 1919 and another set in 1942. During the late '20s, it was featured by Abe Lyman's orchestra, but the great revival took place when the towering trombonist Pee Wee Hunt recorded it with his own small Dixieland band in 1951. Sales soared over the million mark, and jukebox listeners couldn't get their fill. Today it remains a crowd-pleaser.

PIANO or ORGAN SOLO

Moderately bright ragtime tempo

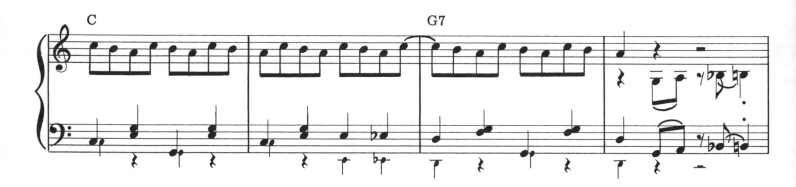

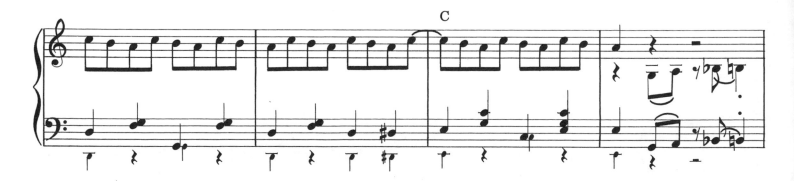

Copyright © 1914, renewed 1941 and assigned to Shapiro, Bernstein & Co. Inc. and Jerry Vogel Music Co., Inc.

K-K-K-KATY

Words and Music by Geoffrey O'Hara

Geoffrey O'Hara, who composed this great World War I comic song, used to delight his vaudeville audiences by performing it in various dialects: French-Canadian, Pidgin English and others. He also wrote church hymns and patriotic songs, and in 1929 he copyrighted "The Star-Spangled Banner" in a low-pitched version because he felt the original key was too high for American voices. It was a gift from this Canadian-born musician to his adopted country.

Jim - my was a sol - dier brave and bold;
No one ev - er looked so nice and neat;

Ka - ty was a maid with hair of gold.
No one could be just as cute and sweet.

Like an act of fate, Kate was
That's what Jim-my thought when the

Copyright © 1918 (renewed 1946) Leo Feist, Inc.

The Lord's Prayer

Music by Albert Hay Malotte

Albert Hay Malotte's setting of "The Lord's Prayer" has resulted in one of the world's most beloved devotional songs. Composed in 1935, the music was in the process of being rejected by a publisher when famed singer John Charles Thomas performed it on a radio broadcast, from the composer's own manuscript. Soon a music dealer in Pittsburgh got so many requests for the sheet music that he phoned in an order for 500 copies to the astounded publisher, who desperately ransacked his mail room to find the score before it could be mailed back to Malotte. Fortunately for all, he did.

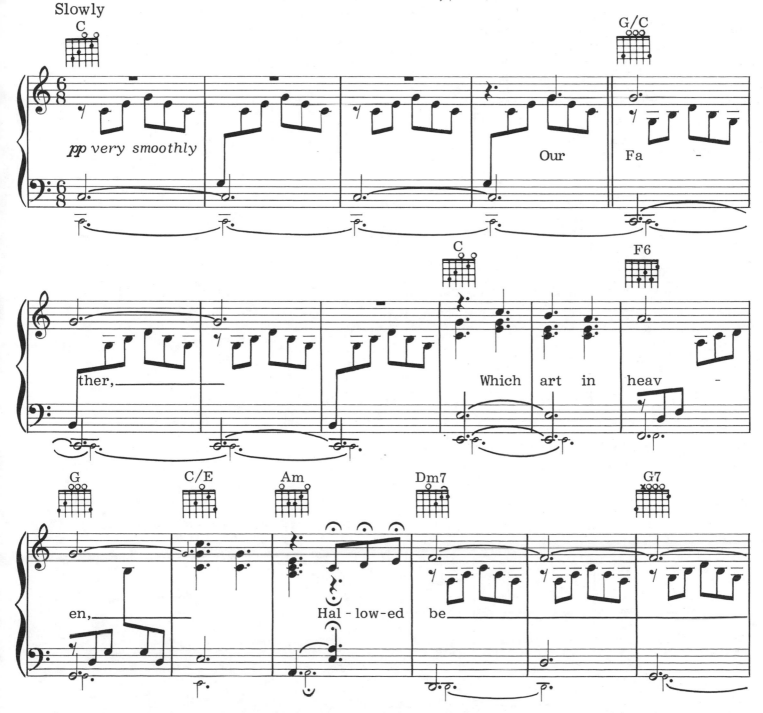

Copyright © 1935 G. Schirmer, Inc.